CREEPY
KENTUCKY

STRANGE STORIES FROM THE BLUEGRASS STATE

KEVEN McQUEEN

THE
History
PRESS

Published by The History Press
Charleston, SC
www.historypress.com

First published 2023

Manufactured in the United States

ISBN 9781467154161

Library of Congress Control Number: 2023937157

For Charles McQueen, the newest member of the tribe.

CONTENTS

Acknowledgements   7

1. Snatched: Louisville Resurrectionists   9
2. Plight of the Living Dead: Premature Burial   26
3. The Tragedy of Lester   33
4. Peculiarly Perishing   38
5. My Old Kentucky (Haunted) Home   55
6. Prognosticated Passings   68
7. Morbid Miscellany   73

Bibliography   103
About the Author   112

ACKNOWLEDGEMENTS

Groveling gratitude goes to:

Eastern Kentucky University Department of English; Eastern Kentucky University Library Express staff; Denise and Amber Hughes; Amy Hawkins McQueen and Quentin Hawkins; Darrell and Swecia McQueen; Darren, Alison, Elizabeth and Charles David McQueen; Kyle McQueen; Michael, Lori and Blaine McQueen and Evan Holbrook; Chad Rhoad, Abigail Fleming and everyone at Arcadia Publishing and The History Press; Craig and Debbie Smith; and Mia Temple. Also: The Healer.

1

SNATCHED

LOUISVILLE RESURRECTIONISTS

There is a physician in this city who is so very skillful that he has been known to have snatched some of his patients from the very grave.
—*editorial joke,* Louisville Courier-Journal, *August 23, 1871*

T he statement may have been in jest, but there was a point: surgeons at medical schools were expected to teach students the fine points of human anatomy, yet for a long time, in Kentucky and other states, the only bodies legally available for study were chiefly furnished by hospitals and jails. There weren't enough anatomical subjects to go around. The *Courier-Journal* noted in 1868 that surgeons had a difficult choice: without bodies to dissect, their medical knowledge was incomplete and they could be sued for malpractice. Yet if they were discovered examining stolen bodies, they could be jailed. Inevitably, body snatching for educational purposes became a lucrative, illegal trade.

Sometimes medical students and/or instructors (or even more likely, school custodians) did the stealing, but most of the time professional grave robbers did the dirty work. These tradesmen's materials were usually impoverished persons buried in potter's fields. As of 1870, in Kentucky the fee was $15 per subject (roughly $280 in modern currency). Sometimes bodies were imported from distant cities, packed in barrels with darkly comic misleading labels such as "pork" or "whisky." Once the merchandise made it to the school, it was embalmed with carbolic acid (cheap!) or sulphate of zinc (expensive!) and stored until needed.

Perhaps Louisville body snatchers were the most industrious in the Commonwealth, as medical schools in the city and in Indiana needed anatomical subjects, and there were so many nearby cemeteries ripe for the plucking. In any case, they left posterity with a trove of medical knowledge and unsavory stories. Here are several, some not for the squeamish.

OUT LIKE FLYNN

Ironworker Thomas Flynn of Eighteenth and Beard Streets was on a drunken spree. He died of an injury on June 5, 1891, at the City Hospital. In the meantime, his wife—who had no idea where he had gone—was unconscious from worry. Flynn's brother-in-law John Moran asked hospital authorities to keep the body until he could determine Mrs. F's wishes for dispensation of the remains. They did so for a few days and then informed Moran he would *have* to make other arrangements hastily. (Why? Hint: it was summertime in the days before easy refrigeration.) Moran and his hardy friends prepared Flynn's body themselves and buried it temporarily in a potter's field. Mrs. Flynn revived on June 10 and said she wanted her poor Thomas to have the best funeral she could afford and burial in the family plot. Undertakers Dougherty and Keenan went to Flynn's putative resting place with shovels only to find him missing. The snatchers would not have won accolades for subtlety: the grave was half unearthed, a mound of recently turned earth was beside it and they abandoned pieces of broken casket. Marks on the ground showed how they dragged Flynn to a wagon. Mrs. Flynn sank back into unconsciousness, and Moran filed a complaint with the authorities. Police went straight to the University of Louisville's medical school, which suggests no one was under any delusions as to the body's whereabouts. The custodian, Ike David, made the lame excuse that he didn't have access to the pickling vat room. Moran and company waited until an unhappy doctor with a key turned up, and after an unpleasant search, they found Flynn in a vat, complete with a hole in his neck wrought by the hook that had pulled him from his grave like a prize-winning salmon. Flynn was reburied in St. John's Cemetery on June 11; at the same time, it was reported that his sickly widow "may not recover from the shock occasioned by the robbery."

A DIFFERENT SORT OF SNATCHER

On February 20, 1894, a fellow calling himself A.E. Brand showed up at the Louisville home of a Black laundress, Frances Gaines, whose son Henry Walker had died there the day before and whose body had not yet been removed. Brand explained that the Masons fraternal order had sent him there to pick up the body. When Gaines expressed healthy skepticism, he said he'd return in the afternoon. There were three small problems with Brand's story: (1) he seemed too roughly dressed to be associated with the Masons; (2) the previous day, three med students had come by Gaines's house and offered to buy Walker's body, to which overture she had sent them packing; (3) and the biggest clue of all, Walker had not been a Mason. A quick investigation uncovered the truth. Brand was just a hobo pretending to be a professional corpse picker-upper. His object was to take Walker's body to the medical school and sell it. He must have known something was up when he came by for the second time hoping to pick up the body and found fifty people staring at him from the yard. He was nearly lynched on the street by a mob of angry Black men before the cops rescued him.

SCHOOL DAYS, GHOUL DAYS

On an evening in early October 1884, a Louisville physician regaled a reporter with a story about an unwholesome incident from when he had been a University of Louisville medical student. Back in December 1879, his roommate—whom he identified only as Dr. K—had taken a dislike to a student from Michigan called "Detroit." Dr. K thought Detroit needed to be taken down a peg. In an ordinary college setting, a snipe hunt might have sufficed or perhaps a hand stealthily immersed in a pitcher of warm water in the dark of night. But this was *medical* school, where students used corpses stolen from their graves for legitimate purposes—also for practical jokes. One evening, the narrator and Dr. K let Detroit know that they were leaving that night to dig up an anatomical subject.

"May I go too?" asked Detroit, rising to the bait.

"No," replied his fellow students. "We don't think you're brave or dependable enough."

"Why, I have the courage of a lion! I know no such thing as fear!" exclaimed Detroit.

"Well…okay," said the others, no doubt with an air suggesting *we are skeptical but willing to give you a chance.*

That night, the expedition consisted of the narrator; Detroit; Dr. K; another student, Dr. P.; and the medical school's custodian Clint, whose duties included helping snatch bodies. Clint and Dr. P also were in on the gag. Evidently, Detroit was quite unpopular. Their destination was a potter's field eight miles from the city where they were to "jerk a stiff" (Clint's phrase) who had died of tuberculosis the day before. Perhaps even Mother Nature herself was a conspirator, for the cold, sleety weather couldn't have been more unpromising (i.e., perfect for the occasion). All the way there, Clint told hair-raising ghost stories to ensure that Detroit would be in a receptive and suggestible mood. The assembled pranksters could tell by the newly tremulous note in Detroit's voice that the stories had taken effect.

At the cemetery, the five-man crew quietly spaded the earth under a weeping willow by the light of a bull's eye lantern. It did not take long to unearth the TB victim, who had been buried two feet below the surface and whose expression was "vicious and hungry, but self-satisfied," as the narrator recalled. As Detroit quaked with ill-concealed fear, his companions tied a rope around the corpse's neck and pulled him out of the grave. The clothing was tossed back in, and the robbers restored the spot to its original appearance. They bagged the unwitting benefactor of science and hid him under the wagon's front seat. Then they sent Clint and Detroit ahead on foot, allegedly to give a signal if necessary.

One thing Detroit did not notice: the resurrectionists had brought *two* sacks. While their mark was occupied, the snatchers put the bag with the body under the wagon's back seat. The narrator crawled into the other bag, which was placed under the front seat where the cadaver previously had been. After a few minutes, they overtook Clint and Detroit, who climbed back into the wagon. Detroit noticed that the narrator was nowhere to be seen and asked where he had gone.

Dr. K said, "Oh, he got out of the wagon and cut through the woods toward the city. It's his turn to be the lookout."

As the conveyance rolled along, Detroit's natural fear of the dead increased by degrees. Finally, to mask his true feelings with a show of bravado, he reached under the front seat, grabbed the "body" and sneered: "Well, damn your old stiff soul, how are you enjoying this ride?"

The narrator sat up quickly in the bag and said politely, in the deepest voice he could muster (try it yourself), "Pretty well, I thank you! How are you enjoying it yourself?" Detroit, a notably snappy dresser, fell overboard in blind panic and landed in ice-cold, slushy mud. His compatriots left him behind, hurrying back to the college to unload their cargo before daybreak.

Detroit showed up at ten o'clock in the morning, sunken-eyed, mud-spattered, speaking strangely and with a noticeable difference in his physical appearance. The narrator recalled that "his hair, which the day before had been as black and glossy as a raven's wing, was now as white as the driven snow." This was perhaps an exaggeration. A day later, Detroit seemed to have largely recovered from his fright, but not long afterward he quit medical school and returned to Michigan. The narrator and Dr. K were sorry afterward and refrained from further practical joking.

The tale's narrator and Dr. P became noted Louisville physicians; Dr. K ditto in Logan County. Presumably, the target of their little jest became a prominent user of hair dye. Clint probably kept on cleaning classrooms and snatching bodies.

A SOUVENIR OF AN INTERESTING OCCASION

The reporter saw a strange photograph in a Louisville physician's office one day in August 1881. It depicted four men in the act of body snatching. One brandished a revolver. Another held an open sack. The third was pulling the body from its hallowed resting place, and the fourth—who looked like the doctor—held a bottle. The doctor was in a reminiscent mood, so he told the journalist about the photo, which was a reminder of an amusing adventure from back in 1875 when he was a medical student—all names withheld, of course!

Three students and the school's janitor had set out in a spring wagon to steal a fresh body. They had directions to the grave, but once there they faced a problem. Beside it was a second, newly dug grave for a man who had died of smallpox. They didn't want to come face to face with the victim of the highly communicable disease, but they weren't certain which grave was which. They thought the plot on the right was the correct one, so they commenced digging in between pulls from a whiskey bottle.

At last, paydirt! When they opened the lid, the narrator saw that the deceased's face was covered with unsightly blotches, a symptom of the dread smallpox. When they removed the body's clothes, the moonlight diagnosis was confirmed. They tossed him back in the grave and refilled it, then dug up the other one. But just as they brought its tenant to the surface, they heard approaching footsteps. After a few tense moments with drawn gun in hand, they realized it was three other medical students out to find another volunteer in a distant section of the cemetery.

So the four snatchers put their body in a sack, loaded it on the wagon, refilled the grave and took off quickly, but not so quickly as to attract unwanted attention. When they were within three miles of the city, the right front wheel of the wagon fell off. Our narrator was pitched onto the road; another student landed on the narrator, and the corpse landed on *him*. Perhaps you have had days like this.

What to do? The delay caused by unearthing the smallpox victim meant that sunrise was in just an hour, and they could hardly risk walking into town with a body in a bag. The doctor recalled, "As a last resort, we determined to let one man drive, and the others walk along beside the wagon and push the wheel on every time it started to come off." Everyone they met gave them suspicious looks, but at last they made it back to the college undetected. So pleased was the group with their feat that they had a photographer take a picture of them posing around the open grave with the tools of their trade:

the gun, the bag, the rope and, perhaps most importantly, the whiskey. Luckily for them, the photographer was less wary than the people they encountered on the road home.

MORRIS IS MISSING

Morris Goldsticker of New York came to Louisville to start a business in 1884. He had an abscess in one ear and entered City Hospital on December 31. He died on New Year's Day 1885. Since no friends or relatives claimed the body, he was buried in a potter's field.

Goldsticker was Jewish, and his employer, S. Hyman, was upset that he had been buried without the proper rituals of his faith. A committee headed by a Mr. Marx obtained a permit to exhume Goldsticker on January 6. When they opened his coffin, which had been buried at a depth of merely three feet, it was empty. The committee vowed to search every medical school, dissecting room and pickling vat in the city.

On January 7, Goldsticker's friends positively identified his body in the dissecting room at the University of Louisville's Medical School. The school made "no resistance," though one wonders what legal defense they could conceivably have offered. Then came a seeming effort on the part of all concerned to hush the matter up, according to the papers: "There seemed to be general desire to smother the affair. [Police Officer Joe] Rosenberg refused to talk about the matter, and Mr. Marx had nothing to say further than the body had been recovered and interred."

IT IS GOOD TO HAVE AMBITION

The December 10, 1885 case of almshouse reject Francis Martzman was different from the usual run of body snatchings in that he wasn't stolen from the grave but right out of the City Hospital's morgue. The impatient ghoul was assumed, probably rightly, to be a medical student, and one in particular was suspected—a fellow who boasted loudly that he *would* snatch a body from the hospital before the winter was over. "Every effort will be made to apprehend the thieves and punish them by a due process of law," said the local papers, but it appears that neither Martzman nor his thief was detected.

THE CORPSE WINS, FOR ONCE

Elderly Louise Coleman, who lived on Tenth Street, knew her remaining days were few in the winter of 1896, but she didn't fear death so much as having her body snatched and dissected by medical students. Her employer, a Miss Saunders, promised she would be decently buried and not pilfered. When Coleman's end came in late February, she was buried in Portland Cemetery. A few days later, her friends found that the grave had been violated.

An investigation found that the dearly departed's niece had the grave opened so she could sell her aunt to a doctor for $15 (a little over $410 in modern currency). The physician protested that he had been swindled. Louise's bones proved so bent and crooked that she was worthless as an anatomical subject. Having taken a bath on that $15 investment, he sent the bones back to Portland Cemetery—but the niece claimed ownership of the plot, which was half full of water anyway, meaning the remains could not be reinterred. They were buried in the potter's field at the doctor's expense. In all, his adventure with Louise Coleman's corpse cost him $25 (in modern currency, $795).

We learn, as a sidelight to this case, that medical colleges of the era sometimes *rented* bodies if the supply was low. The schools would borrow a body from an undertaker, dissect all of it except the face and then send it back in time for the funeral.

BONE APPÉTIT

Readers of my book *Offbeat Kentuckians* may remember Simon Kracht, the University of Louisville medical school janitor who doubled as the institution's grave robber. Kracht was even photographed brandishing a shovel and a bag of bones, such was his sauciness. A resurrectionist's life was full of hilarious incidents such as this: on June 5, 1874, Simon's fifteen-year-old daughter Julia made soup for dinner. She saw water in a barrel and thought it useful for cookery. But she didn't know that the water had been sitting for months and that it was the same barrel her father used to haul around bodies and anatomical bits and pieces. To make matters worse, doctors and students washed their hands in it after pickling the dead or cutting up the same. Traces of arsenic (used as a preservative), pieces of skin, bits of bone and God knows what commingled in the soup's broth

along with wholesome ingredients. A student heard shouts and entered the Kracht home to find father, mother, daughter and son writhing in agony. Luckily, the dispensary was near and everyone got an antidote. But Simon's hairbreadth reprieve from the reaper's chilly embrace was temporary. The next year, he died by suicide.

ROEDEMER, WANDERER

The *Courier-Journal* drew attention to an outbreak of "heartless" university medical students robbing graves in summer 1871. "The rights of the quick and the dead have been outraged," said the paper, though the students would have argued that the deceased have no "rights" in the usual sense. The police, realizing it would be too difficult to stake out every graveyard in the vicinity, watched the medical school's entrances. Their patience paid off on the night of August 5, when they stopped a suspicious wagon after firing two warning shots in the air. Dialogue something like the following ensued:

Cops: "There's a coffin in your wagon."

Driver: "It's empty."

Cops: "But there's a piece of red flannel sticking out."

Driver: "That's to keep the lid from rubbing."

Cops: "The reek that issues from this receptacle for the dead is offensive to the olfactory organ."

Driver: "It's empty, I tell ya!"

Suspicious, no? But when officers opened the lid—lo, it *was* empty. The driver, whose name was Granville W. Smith, wrote an indignant letter about the incident, printed in the *Courier-Journal* on August 7. It ended with this parting shot: "I have been engaged in the coffin business in this city off and on for the last twenty years and never have I yet seen a watchman until the other night that did not know an undertaker's wagon."

It was like a drug bust gone bad, only involving a casket instead of drugs, but a month later Adam Roedemer had his elderly brother George's coffin exhumed and found it empty. The disappearance provoked a citywide sensation, and the *Courier-Journal* was flooded with over one hundred letters from citizens, mostly bitter denunciations of the medical profession. The heat was on, and somebody somewhere decided it was wise to ditch the stolen property. On the night of September 9, a policeman found the badly emaciated but undissected body in a coffee sack in the alley between Fourth and Center Streets. Considering that this location was behind the Louisville Medical College and that the body was pickled in brine, this was hardly the cleverest dump site. He was identified as the missing two-weeks-deceased George Roedemer and buried in Western Cemetery.

The theft must have made an impression, since the *Courier-Journal* was still harping on it three years later in an editorial revealing that the deceased was re-snatched: "[T]he doctors managed to get the body again, and it was mutilated by the dissecting knife, and science was benefitted in the proper degree thereby."

A HILARIOUS YARN

Circa 1855, the Louisville University's School of Medicine had an employee whose chief task was plucking cadavers from the tomb and bringing them back for doctors. This craftsman heard a rumor one day that a body was floating in a canal. He rushed to the location before the police arrived and stuffed his prize in a sack, which required the snatcher to bend the corpse into a horseshoe shape. The snatcher hid the bag, but when he retrieved it later, rigor mortis had set in. Our undaunted hero took it to the medical school despite its funny position. When the snatcher stretched out on the floor for a hard-earned nap and pleasant dreams about full, unguarded graveyards with thin soil, the janitor built a fire so the body would thaw out. As it limbered up, the corpse started twitching. The janitor thought it would be funny to scare the snatcher, so he woke up the sleeping fellow and pointed at the body, which seemed on the verge of writhing out of the sack. Rather than being frightened, the snatcher was angry, feeling that he had been cheated somehow. He grabbed the body by the throat and was about to beat its brains out with a blunt object when the janitor hastily explained that it was all just a gag.

FINGER FOOD

Speaking of practical jokes and body snatchers, in January 1876 Louisville medical students dissected a body. One of them, a fellow with a sparkling sense of humor, cut off a finger and put it in his pocket just in case he

should think of a good practical joke to play with it. Inspiration came when he saw a plate of free sausages in a saloon. He hid the digit among the savory morsels and just waited for someone to come along and take a bite. That someone was a cop on his beat, who gnawed on the supposed sausage until he apprehended that it had a fingernail. It was all intended to be a harmless joke, but the officer had no idea where the laugh was supposed to come in.

THE LEGAL SYSTEM FAILS MR. GILHANY

Francis Gilhany, a Cincinnati shoemaker, was visiting Louisville when he died at City Hospital on January 22, 1857. On January 27, the brother of the deceased came to the city to have the body exhumed and sent home. Gilhany's grave proved empty, and his indignant brother applied for a search warrant.

The number one snatching suspect was City Hospital's graveyard sexton Peter Weimans. Testimony in court proved that while the late Gilhany had been taken to Cave Hill Cemetery, he was stashed in a corncrib rather than buried. Where did he go? No witnesses claimed to know, and Weimans vowed to press a charge of false imprisonment against Gilhany's brother.

Weimans was discharged on February 6. That's how most lawsuits against alleged body snatchers ended. "Smoking gun" evidence could not be found, having long since been dissected and disposed of, and a defunct human body didn't belong to anyone, technically speaking.

WE NO HABEAS CORPUS

In December 1869, the body of an elderly stranger was found frozen stiff in the forest at Middletown, near Louisville. A bag of tools suggested he was a tinker (a traveling repairman of household items). A magistrate held an inquest. There seemed to be no visible signs of violence, so the jury ruled that he met his maker via exposure to the elements. He was buried in the potter's field.

A local doctor who taught medical classes on the side exhumed the unknown and friendless wayfarer. However, when students took a closer look at the corpse's head, they found small holes indicating that their subject was murdered. The jury had been wrong! Now the doctor and his students were in a predicament: if they reported the crime, they would get in serious trouble for body snatching. But if they didn't tell the authorities, a killer might walk unpunished. They decided to save their own hides and swore each other to secrecy. Nevertheless, the story got out and became the subject of a *Courier-Journal* article in March 1870.

Further investigation proved that the dead man was Frank Hanks and he had been a clock repairman. He was known to have $150 and a gold watch before he disappeared, neither of which was found on his body, strongly suggesting robbery as a motive for murder. Suspicion fell on a Middletown man who suddenly, inexplicably became flush with money after Hanks died. But the prime piece of evidence—the body—was long since dissected into a state of uselessness. If charges were ever filed against the prime suspect, the record fails to disclose it.

SNATCHED AND SOAKED

On the night of November 28, 1868, three Louisville medical students boarded a yawl and rowed across to Indiana to snatch a convict at New Albany. The usual procedure was to abstract the body and leave the coffin, but in this case distant footsteps panicked the students and they took the casket with them. They loaded it on their boat and headed for Louisville. But just above the falls, the yawl capsized and the students had to swim for it—but not before they were treated to a vision seen by very few. The coffin lid burst and out came their prize, upright with rigor mortis, face of milky white, eyes and mouth wide open and clinging to their capsized boat. The sopping wet and chilled students made it to shore, where they watched the prisoner floating away in the river fog, sure to surprise whoever found him.

THUMB 'N' A RIDE

On December 4, 1872, careless ghouls dropped a detached thumb on the street in Louisville, which attracted much unfavorable comment and heightened the populace's awareness. Two nights later, officers walking their beat on Eighth and Chestnut Streets stopped a wagon at the rear of the medical college. The cargo proved to be two dead men, and an inspection of the school uncovered two already-delivered dead women. The drivers of the wagon—a student and the institution's janitor—were arrested. The student was fined and discharged, and the janitor likely fared no worse. In the meanwhile, the cadavers were taken to the police station house. There they stayed until the city reburied them, but not before throngs of Louisvillian trooped through the building to see them. Three of the four bodies were African American, and many Black spectators were quick to suspect that the would-be anatomical subjects had been murdered.

HAPPILY CADAVER AFTER

The state legislature had an opportunity to rectify the body snatching problem in the spring of 1873, when a bill recommended that medical schools be given the bodies of paupers whose burials "would be a public charge." For reasons unexplained, the bill was rejected by a majority, and one assumes that when election time rolled around again, politicians accused one another of being soft on grave robbery. Thus the issue continued for at least another twenty years.

Some people understandably objected to their remains being snatched, as illustrated by Louisvillian Jennie Robinson's will, dated May 16, 1902: "It is my request that in case I should die at any time and there should be any probability of the students obtaining my body, I desire that [it] be placed in a vault until after a sufficient time has elapsed that there will be no danger of them getting my body."

I don't know if Jennie's plan worked, but resurrectionists kept stealing the gone away long after one might think it necessary for furthering the ends of science. A body snatching scare erupted across the Midwest in the autumn and winter of 1902 after the arrest of industrious grave robber/ murderer Rufus Cantrell (see my History Press book *Forgotten Tales of Indiana* for details), and Louisville was not immune, since it was rumored that Cantrell had attained wholesale goods there. In early December, the *Courier-Journal* ran a three-part article demanding answers from medical schools' staff.

Kentucky law since 1894 held that after three days, the bodies of the indigent would be turned over to medical colleges; also, bodies were to be preserved but not dissected for thirty days in case someone should belatedly claim them. Nevertheless, it was common knowledge by 1902 that University of Louisville physicians and their students had been lifting bodies from the hospital morgue, a subtler method than undergoing the backbreaking toil and danger of unearthing a grave. The snatchers raided the fridge—so to speak—even when friends and relatives of the dead forbade it. The *Courier-Journal* mentioned two recent cases. Nathan B. Walker, formerly well-to-do but fallen on hard times, died on November 24, 1902. Newspaper editor Henry Watterson's secretary G.E. Johnson became suspicious when denied entrance to the city morgue in the university hospital despite a clear order from the city's Board of Public Safety, dating from September 1895, that "the dead house should be kept open always." (Although the morgue was supposed to be open to the public, the university treated it as their own private institution, a "cold storage plant" for bodies awaiting dissection. Neither citizens nor officers of the law were given admission.)

Johnson became even warier when a Dr. Gilbert said Johnson would be charged five bucks to haul Walker away, and gee, wouldn't it just be easier to let the medical school have the poor fellow? The doctor repeated this entreaty three times. Finally, Dr. Gilbert admitted that Walker's body was not in the morgue but rather had been commandeered by a pool of dissectors. Then, surely enough, Dr. Gilbert charged Johnson five big ones for the expense of embalming, hauling and storing Walker, though they had done these actions without permission. At least the physician gave Johnson a receipt worthy of framing as a unique memento. And even after paying hard cash, he didn't receive Walker for three days.

In the other 1902 case, George Melton accidentally shot his wife, Martha, then requested undertaker Bax to retrieve her from the hospital. Bax found that the body had already been hustled off to the morgue without authority, and the officials could only cough and say that the institution's body-handling assistants mistook her for another corpse. This seemed unlikely, as the *other* body was a man, and Melton had a distinctive gunshot wound and surgical incisions.

The *Courier-Journal* noted that several Black citizens complained that they had been unable to pick up the bodies of relatives who died at the hospital, contrary to law. The paper observed, "The medical colleges of Louisville have never legally acquired a single dead body from the public institutions since the passage of the law in 1894." The law maintained that professors receiving cadavers should give a $1,000 penal bond to be approved by the county court clerk, but a survey of the records showed that not one bond had ever been given, although surgeons violating the law could be fined up to $1,000. Two doctors claimed that they had put up a bond in 1894, but the clerk could find no record. "We have the receipt in our office, and we will be back in an hour with it," the doctors said as they inched toward the door. They didn't return.

Reporters questioned attorneys, who said that "the medical colleges have laid themselves liable to damages for every body they have taken from the public institutions since the law went into effect." Physicians connected with the hospitals each claimed *someone else* was in charge of the legalities, not a good sign.

To put it in layman's terms, somebody was potentially in trouble. But medical knowledge itself also was in peril. Thanks to the bad publicity, it was reported on December 3 that the city's supply of subjects was running low, resulting in what the *Courier-Journal* drolly called a "famine of cadavers." An upperclassman complained that only thirty bodes remained. Suddenly, the price of a fresh, undissected body jumped to fifty dollars. We are not given to know what happened next, but the law of supply and demand probably meant that some men who weren't afraid of getting their hands dirty dusted off their shovels, just like in the old days of thirty years before.

In time, medical schools in Kentucky and elsewhere got their fill of subjects and grave robbing became a lost folk art. In December 1922, columnist Will S. Kaltenbacher stated, "It has been a long time since a grave robbery was reported in Kentucky, and the ghouls, if their reported operations were as extensive as was believed, evidently have taken up a less gruesome occupation."

2

PLIGHT OF THE LIVING DEAD

PREMATURE BURIAL

O ur ancestors were obsessed with being prematurely buried. It was a very real possibility. It is impossible to tell how many people suffered this dreadful fate, since there is generally no good reason to unearth a casket and most confirmed cases were discovered by accident, such as when bodies were exhumed for intended reburial. Edgar Allan Poe wrote a humorous story on the topic called "Loss of Breath," in which the protagonist loses his power to breathe on his honeymoon and is mistaken for dead, after which his sentient "corpse" is tossed out of a moving stagecoach, hanged when mistaken for a criminal, mutilated by a coroner and disemboweled by a pharmacist. Well, it was funny if you were Edgar Allan Poe.

Old newspapers teem with real-life examples of people who were fortuitously rescued and others who weren't. Here are many examples of yesteryear's Kentuckians having close calls with a horrifying fate and gaining a renewed appreciation for life and oxygen:

THE NINETEENTH CENTURY SAW repeated outbreaks of cholera, a disease so virulent that its victims were generally buried as quickly as possible to prevent further contagion. However, it so closely mimicked death that untold numbers of cholera victims were buried alive—a predicament memorably depicted in Belgian artist Antoine Wiertz's nightmare-inducing 1854 painting *The Premature Burial*. During the 1833 epidemic that struck most of America, a Mrs. Williams of Fleming County slipped into a deathlike state. The grave was dug, and she was dressed in her winding sheet with great haste. But she hadn't died much after all. Just as the attendants were screwing down the lid, she mustered strength to knock feebly. They gave Williams restoratives, and she fully recovered. She was alive forty years later, when a newspaper correspondent told her unsettling tale to the *Carlisle Mercury*.

IN AUGUST 1849, AN unnamed German seemingly died of cholera aboard the steamboat *Cambria* during a voyage from Cincinnati to St. Louis. The ship's crew (and no doubt the passengers) wanted the man buried ashore as quickly as possible. However, Captain Kendrick ordered them to make certain. Eight hours later, the captain found the German cold to the touch. The ship docked near Hawesville in Hancock County, Kentucky. Laborers dug a grave and carried the coffin to it. But just before the lid was closed to the sunlight forever, the not-so-dead German opened his eyes and gasped. He made a full recovery, but the ship's carpenter who made the coffin fell ill, died and was buried the next day. Let's hope they waited a while first.

JOHN NETHERTON OF FLOYDSBURG, Oldham County, seemed to have died of smallpox in April 1869 after a nine days' illness. His nurses left his bedside to order a first-class grave digging. When they returned, they found that despite Netherton's death, he got better. He lived quite a while after his close scrape, dying on June 14, 1873.

CHARLES BROWN, WHO LIVED near Stamping Ground, Scott County, died in February 1876, and the usual ritual was followed: he was placed in a coffin and prepared to be buried the next day. But his alleged death didn't "take," and during the night, his eyes opened and he started feeling much better. The next day he was "as well and hearty as he ever was," said the *Georgetown Times*. The practical Brown kept the coffin, saying he'd have use for it eventually.

ON APRIL 21, 1876, a Black laborer for the Louisville, Paducah and Southwestern Railroad fell off a moving handcar at Princeton, Caldwell County. Roadmaster John Witty and the worker's companions examined the body and declared him deceased though he had no visible injuries, believing he had broken his neck. He was taken to the station house, and Witty queried the Louisville office via telegraph as to dispensation of the remains. The answer came next day: "Have the body brought up to Elizabethtown; get an undertaker and have it decently buried on account of the L., P., and S.W.R.R." Witty replied that the "dead man" had revived several hours after his accident; the laborer said he "didn't want to be buried" and would be back at work on Monday with a shovel and hoe, and he added with refreshing humor that he was better than a dozen dead men.

LAURA RATHFIELD (NAME ALSO given as Rothfield and Rothfeld), age seventeen and "a rather good-looking young girl of pleasing exterior," had an epileptic fit at her home on East Green Street, Louisville, on November 24, 1876. She died on Wednesday, November 29. The doctor had her beshrouded and encoffined. But was she *really* dead? That's what her mother and other doctors couldn't quite figure out. Yes, she was "lifeless and cold" and not breathing. However, on Thursday afternoon, witnesses said Laura's lips moved and her waxy pallor flushed to pink. A family story held that Laura's grandmother also had fallen into a deathlike coma when young and recovered fully after two days, so the girl's mother clung to the hope that history was repeating itself. The minister of the German Lutheran church came to see for himself and declared that she was merely in a trance. At his recommendation, Laura was placed on a lounge until the matter could be settled with certainty. It could do no good if she revived and found herself in a casket. A fire was lit to keep Laura warm.

The poet Alexander Pope once asked, "Who shall decide when doctors disagree?" And that includes pronouncing death. Dr. Krim examined Laura and argued that she bore the classic symptoms of death: sunken eyes, pale face, blue lips, rigid limbs. However, another doctor thought she might still be alive. Starting Friday evening, Laura's midsection became soft and warm rather than stiff and cold—or was that just the result of being close to a fire?—but the rest of her body remained frigid. The family swore that her lips were open Friday afternoon, closed Friday evening and parted again Saturday morning. On Friday, her right cheek took on a "blackish hue," but it went away. Most intriguing, there was no odor of decomposition although she had been dead, or perhaps "dead," for three days. "The physicians who have been at the house seem to think that death can be seen, but some circumstances make them hesitate in being positive," wrote a reporter. They advised that Laura not be buried yet, just in case.

Sunday, December 3: No material change, though Laura allegedly opened and closed her mouth several times. Doctors remained in the room around the clock.

Monday, December 4: The body was warm and the lips "healthy and red." Nevertheless, doctors were certain Laura was dead. Her family, on the other hand, was so sure she was alive that they took down the funerary crape on their door. Hundreds of busybodies came by to gawk but were turned away.

Tuesday, December 5: Still no change in Laura's condition.

Wednesday, December 6: Pungent and undeniable evidence of death finally commenced, and Laura was placed in a cemetery vault the same day.

MRS. SHIFLET, AN OCTOGENARIAN, died at her home twelve miles from Richmond, Madison County, on January 23, 1882. Her daughter, who lived in the city, had a casket with all the trimmings packed, placed in a hearse and sent to Shiflet's house. On the way, however, the hearse's driver was stopped by a messenger coming from the opposite direction, who told him the elderly woman was reviving and his wares would not be needed. The journalist who related the near-miss with premature burial noted that Shiflet's sister had undergone a similar experience years before and still flourished.

CARRIE C. RINGOLD, MANUFACTURER of artificial flowers, lived in a charming red cottage with green shutters on the east side of Louisville's Jackson Street, between Market and Jefferson. She died there, too, on January 24, 1885, or so Dr. Beutel said. He declared that she had fallen victim to heart disease. Her waxy pallor and fixed, staring eyes seemed to confirm it.

All day on January 25, friends and relatives trooped by the coffin and paid homage. Perhaps some of the mourners nervously remembered some remarkable (in more ways than one) incidents from the dearly departed's past: at age thirteen, she had married a man named Thatcher. During the honeymoon period, she went into a seven-month trance. When she finally revived, she married a Mr. Snyder—presumably, Thatcher had divorced his unconscious wife—but seven months later she deserted Snyder and returned to Thatcher, only to leave him three years later and marry a Mr. Clearen. Soon afterward, she lapsed into a second trance, this one lasting seven weeks. A grave was dug and the minister was exhorting when she snapped out of it, escaping premature burial again, this time by mere minutes.

After this adventure, she married her fourth husband, Ringold, and here she was, dead again. The burial was scheduled for January 26, but then history seemed to repeat itself for the third time. Her lips turned red, her cheeks regained their color and she turned slightly in her coffin. Dr. Beutel was recalled. He agreed that she appeared to be showing outward signs of life, but her heart was motionless.

By nightfall, she still retained a lifelike appearance in her face but her body had started mortifying, and how. Dr. Beutel declared her dead, her friends quickly agreed and she was buried in Cave Hill Cemetery under her maiden name, Carrie C. Young, on January 27.

GEORGE O. DANIELS DIED after a long illness on Wednesday, June 16, 1886, at his home in Clinton, Hickman County. His relatives gathered on Thursday to pay their respects. At midnight, they heard "a deep groan" issuing from within the coffin's snug confines. The understandably worried relatives exited the premises on the double quick, but luckily for Daniels, a German neighbor named Wabbeking opened the lid and pulled the occupant upright into a sitting position. The family gradually returned when they thought it safe, and Daniels said he had been aware of everything that occurred since his "death" but had been unable to move a muscle or speak a word.

ANNIE WATKINS, ELDERLY AND Black, died in Paducah, McCracken County, on August 6, 1887. Neighbors gathered for the funeral on August 7. But the wake turned out to be a waking! Annie sat up in her coffin, and the mourners flew like wing-footed Hermes. White neighbor ladies provided first aid, and Watkins spent August 8 not underground in a coffin but participating in an emancipation celebration.

GEORGE NICHOLAS HAWES, SON of Judge Richard Hawes, seemed to have died during the cholera epidemic of 1849 in Paris, Bourbon County. He revived just before the undertaker screwed down the coffin lid. Hawes made a full recovery and died in Millersburg, nearly forty years later, on March 25, 1888, at age sixty-five.

A "HIGHLY ESTEEMED CITIZEN" (whose name the journalist withheld) of Monroe County went into a state of suspended animation during an illness circa January 1894. His doctor and friends thought he died and laid his body out for burial. Suddenly his eyes flipped open, and he informed the very interested spectators that he had been in hell (evidently), but it wasn't such a bad place at that: "The flames were not so severe as he expected." Several hours later, he died for real. Adding to the strangeness, his experience paralleled the adventure of another Monroe Countian named Dunham a few years before. Dunham seemingly died and then astounded his grieving friends by jumping out of his bed and locking himself in a closet. He explained that he had just visited the nether regions and didn't want to return. His friends sweet-talked him into getting back into his deathbed, where he expired a day later. "The truth of both these statements can be vouched for by the very best of citizens," concluded the reporter who related them. Whether the detail about the tolerably sultry afterlife is true or not, both men easily could have been buried alive had they not revived in time.

MRS. S.S. DICKERMAN REPORTEDLY died on October 11, 1903, at Bryantsville, Garrard County. But she fooled everyone good! After being laid out for viewing for twenty-fours, she was within one hour of being buried when someone noticed signs of life returning.

JOSEPHINE HUNKLER OF BELLEVUE, Campbell County, died of dropsy around March 11, 1904. Nearby relatives even heard her death rattle. But she revived two hours later. That was the good news. The bad news was that "the transitory stage dethroned her mind," as the papers said.

JANE TAYLOR'S NEIGHBORS IN Henderson were dressing her for burial on February 8, 1907. She spoke to them although she had been pronounced dead the night before. Posterity does not record exactly what she said, but probably it was something like "What do you think you're doing?"

PARKER ROBINSON WAS MINDING his own business eating lunch on a Lexington Street restaurant in Versailles, Woodford County, on November 18, 1912, when he toppled over. His heart rate and pulse were nil, so off to the undertaker with him. The coroner was on the way when Robinson sat up and inquired about the change in his surroundings. "A good deal of excitement was caused," remarked a press account.

BURGET HILL WAS OFFICIALLY pronounced dead at Shelbyville, Shelby County, on the morning of September 17, 1916. Undertaker Guy Wells was just about to embalm when Hill started breathing. A doctor provided ministrations, but Hill died a second, more permanent, time three hours later.

3

THE TRAGEDY OF LESTER

Fourteen-year-old Lester Bryant, son of William A. Bryant, was the pride of Rockfield, a small town in Warren County near Bowling Green. He was crowned the "Champion Corn Grower" of the state in 1912. He grew 148 bushels and 55 pounds of corn on only one acre of land. It cost him slightly over $0.12 a bushel, leaving him a net profit of $70.25. To put it in a modern perspective, this would be like spending $364 and making a profit of $1,440. He also won $300 in prizes ($6,160 in modern currency).

The *Louisville Courier-Journal* of January 14, 1913, featured a photo of Lester posing with his proud teacher, Miss Calcie Haynes, of the Cave Springs rural school.

The Commercial Club of Louisville was so impressed with Lester's feat that they sent him on a free five-day trip to Washington, D.C., where he would meet like-minded youths from across the nation, after which they were to attend a meeting of the National Boys' Corn Growing Association in Columbia, South Carolina. He spent January 18, 1913, in Louisville as a guest of the Commercial Club. Next day he left for the nation's capital.

"The paths of glory lead but to the grave," said Thomas Gray in "Elegy Written in a Country Churchyard," and this sad truth applies even to champion corn growers. In retrospect, it would have been better for Lester Bryant if he had not won the state's admiration for his agricultural wizardry.

On the afternoon of January 20, a few hours after Lester reached D.C., he was found dead in his rented room, "the victim of ignorance and frugality," in the words of the *Courier-Journal*. The Department of Agriculture had instructed Lester to stay with the other winners at the Ebbitt House hotel. However, to save money, he went instead to a cheapo rooming house at 301 Delaware Avenue. He made a second critical mistake by leaving the train station before his welcoming committee arrived.

That was the frugality; as for the ignorance, Lester was unfamiliar with big-city technology and did not know how to operate the gas lighting fixtures in his room. He blew out the gas like a candle on a birthday cake and thought that was sufficient, but did not turn off the gas jet. The room lacked signs warning guests not to blow the light out. Gas filled the room as the oxygen supply dwindled. At some point, Lester must have realized his peril, as he was found facedown on the floor as though he were trying to reach the door. The coroner confirmed that he asphyxiated.

Meanwhile, agents from the Department of Agriculture were frantically searching the city for him, as he was not in the Ebbitt House, where they assumed he would be. They found him at the undertaker's. He was identified by his corn club button.

Lester was sent home to Rockfield via train and buried in Bowling Green's Fairview Cemetery on January 22. Six schoolmates were his pallbearers. The Department of Agriculture sent a floral arrangement. Even the silver plate on Lester's coffin reminded all of his title: "Champion Corn Grower."

Politicians and newspapers reacted to Lester's untimely death with the sort of encomia one would expect to be reserved for statesmen or war heroes—in fact, it was the sort of obituary soldiers would receive when the Great War started next year. It may seem strange to us for a farm boy to receive so much adulation, but Kentucky was very much an agrarian state and contributors to agriculture were considered useful members of society. No less a personage than the secretary of state sent a letter to Warren County school superintendent Emory White informing him that Bryant had posthumously won a silver trophy for making the largest profit from an acre of land. Representative A.B. Rouse said: "I never saw a finer, sturdier specimen of boyhood….Every inch of him was fit and powerful. It was one of the most tragic and pitiful endings to a life of promise I ever heard of." Lester was given a lengthy and elaborate eulogy in Congress by Representative Heflin of Alabama.

From a *Courier-Journal* editorial: "Lester Bryant's labor was worth much to his county and his example was worth much to the state. His untimely death is a loss not only to his parents…but, in some degree, a loss to the Commonwealth and to the country at large."

The *Owensboro Messenger*: "There was the making evidently of a fine man in Lester Bryant….He had shown what could be done on Kentucky soil by proper cultivation."

Bowling Green Times-Journal: "In a sense he belonged to the citizens in general, and his tragic death brings sorrow to all….He accomplished far more for the county in which he was born and reared than do many who live to a ripe age."

Owensboro Inquirer: "He had exhibited that pluck and energy which clearly demonstrated the development of a man who would do things in the world."

The *Lexington Herald* waxed poetic: "If his example abide and other boys learn the lesson his busy career impressed, he will not have lived in vain, and each returning autumn when the yellow banners of the corn, in unnumbered fields, have waved goodbye to the summer of his useful life….These will be his monument."

Some people blamed Uncle Sam, thinking the government did not do enough to protect its charge when he arrived in D.C. Thundered Representative R.Y. Thomas Jr.:

> *The Department of Agriculture will have to give me absolute proof that this boy was not neglected. They appear to have done everything in their power to locate him* [and] *to have provided definite instructions* [where to go when he arrived in the city]. *But I am going to examine them thoroughly and, if I find that there was neglect, someone is going to suffer for it. I am going to find out what sort of rooming house he stopped in, whether there were proper placards in it about turning off the gas and, if not, why not.*

The *Courier-Journal* agreed: "It is not sufficient to know that he was not met at the station. Why was he overlooked? By whom was he overlooked? Whose fault was it that this child, a stranger to the ways of cities, was allowed to shift for himself and meet with a fatal accident? He was a guest of the federal government. As such he was entitled to the fullest protection."

Said the *Bowling Green News*: "It looks very much like the committee at Washington appointed to look after the interest of Lester Bryant had been remiss in their duty, else he would not be a corpse today."

The *Bowling Green Messenger*: "It is not to be supposed that a boy of fifteen [*sic*], who had probably never spent a day away from home until this trip, should have known of the environs of Washington. It was almost criminal to have sent him alone to one of the large cities without protection."

It is hard to see how the government could be at fault if Lester refused to follow the detailed directions he was sent, but it is human nature for people to blame *someone* when they are angry. The secretary of the Department of Agriculture announced on January 23 that he had made a thorough investigation: "I have come to the conclusion that the department did everything in its power to meet and care for Lester Bryant. His death is to be regretted, and no one regrets it more than the department, but we feel that we are blameless in the matter."

O.H. Benson of the farm management division similarly noted that while the department was heartbroken over Bryant's loss, it would have been avoided if he had gone to Ebbitt House as he was told or waited at the train depot until officials came to greet him—as he also had been directed. Since Bryant was not at the station when his greeters showed up, they thought he had missed his train and would arrive on a later one. Benson even released to the press the instruction letter that had been mailed to all champion corn club winners.

Before the month was over, a movement started in Bowling Green to raise a hero's memorial for Lester. The matter was taken up in Washington but rejected on the grounds that while the representatives' motives in introducing the legislation were noble, if it passed Congress would be inundated with pleas for private monument money.

So citizens did what they ought to do in the first place in situations such as this: they raised the money themselves. Professor Fred Mutchler of the Western State Normal School at Bowling Green selected fifty bushels of corn grown by Lester. The ears were peddled for a dollar apiece.

Six hundred ears of sold corn later, on August 15, 1914, a six-foot-high monument to Lester was erected in Fairview Cemetery. Of course, it did not fail to mention his claim to fame: "State Champion Corn Grower—1912. Record 148 bu. 55 lbs. on one acre." There is a melancholy quatrain:

> *The hoe that he wielded will be covered with dust,*
> *The plow that he guided be still;*
> *The trace chains be red with rust,*
> *While he sleeps on the slope of the hill.*

And appropriately, an ear of corn is carved near the top.

Is the moral of the story to *avoid* hard work and frugality, since these qualities arguably led to Lester Bryant's demise? Or is it to work hard but also follow directions? Your answer might say something about your personality.

4

PECULIARLY PERISHING

LAST WORDS: "ARF ARF"

David Bailey of Bath County had two related failings: he liked to get drunk, and while in that condition he enjoyed growling like a dog. One night, Bailey indulged in both pastimes too near George Shout's house. The homeowner thought he heard a rabid dog and stepped outside with a loaded shotgun. "Git!" shouted Shout. "Rrrrrr!" answered Bailey. A jury acquitted Shout in March 1873.

HEARTLESS OBITUARIES

Charles Crosby was married for only one day in the Louisville suburb of Germantown in January 1843. The *Journal* explains why: "Not fancying the noose into which he had slipped his neck, he soon looked out for a better one. He hung himself on the first day of the honeymoon."

In a fit of jealousy, German cigar maker Louis Buets shot himself in the head in his Louisville residence on July 9, 1854. His death announcement read, "So much for love and powder."

Mr. Lough of Pendleton County made the inadvisable choice of carrying his brand-new, needle-sharp axe under his overcoat as he rode home in early 1855. By the time he got there, the axe-head had worked its way into his side. Lough's obituary struck a strangely incredulous tone: "Was ever the like heard of?"

Jacob Hascher walked onto the Ohio River bridge at Louisville and shot himself in the head on August 14, 1875. But what the *Courier-Journal*'s headline writer couldn't understand was why Hascher spent a few pennies on a bullet when he had a free means of surceasing his sorrows: "He Could Have Drowned Cheaper."

Charles Talbot Pierce hanged himself in Louisville on November 12, 1918, by jumping off an inverted bucket. His obit couldn't resist pointing out the obvious cliché: "Workman at Camp Knox Literally Kicks Bucket."

WILLIAM GETS LUCKY!

William Parr, who lived three miles from Lexington, Fayette County, received news that he had inherited a fortune from a British relative. Parr embraced his good fortune by going on a bender lasting several days, hopping into a wagon with a loaded pistol and vowing to annihilate anyone who came near him. He intentionally stayed out in the rain until he caught pneumonia, which terminated fatally on July 30, 1875.

CURRENT EVENTS

Nineteenth-century Kentucky superstition maintained that lightning would not strike beech trees. On July 19, 1842, William Bell, Jesse Hays, Gabriel Scresely and Charles Taylor proved conclusively that the belief had no foundation at Mount Washington, Bullitt County.

In 1853, Walter Dodson was merely stunned when a bolt from the blue killed a nearby son of A. Toner. But the lightning gods were not to be thwarted. On August 6, 1860, Dodson was in a carpenter's shop in Flemingsburg, Fleming County, with Toner's second son when lightning killed Dodson. This Toner escaped with minor injuries.

V. Bowen and John Debaun were candidates for the office of Mercer County jailer. They were both killed by lightning at the same time on July 24, 1866, which means the county had to find two new candidates.

GETTING HIS KICKS

Harlin Collins and his pal Delmer were walking home from Caintown, Pulaski County, on the night of November 21, 1916, when they encountered a mule.

"I dare you to kick it!" said Collins.

"No thanks," replied Delmer.

"Well, I'll take a chance," countered Collins, who then found that while mules dearly enjoy kicking the stuffin' out of other beings, they dish it out better than they take it. Doctors said Collins's prognosis was not encouraging.

WELL TRAINED

Railroad brakeman W.L. Tackett craved a nap early in the morning of August 30, 1918. He stretched out on the ground at Jenkins, Letcher County, and used a railroad tie for a presumably uncomfortable pillow. Let's just say he must have been a sound sleeper and leave it at that.

FLAT BROKE

James Brooks, age nineteen, was convicted of vagrancy and sentenced to spend ten days in Louisville's workhouse. On May 10, 1921, Brooks goofed off by hiding in an empty bin. It *was* a great idea, until tons of crushed rocks came barreling through the chute.

MCLAUGHLIN'S METHOD ACTING

J.J. McLaughlin of Hopkinsville, Christian County, was a budding lawyer and amateur actor "of fine personal appearance, great dramatic talent, and energy of character." On March 26, 1835, he was taking the lead role in Charles Maturin's 1816 tragedy *Bertram, or: The Castle of St. Aldobrand* in Nashville. He told his fellow thespians, "I will play Bertram as it never has been played on those boards." An editor reminiscing in 1848 remarked with understatement, "He kept his word."

In the fifth act, the character Bertram stabs himself to death, but McLaughlin forgot to bring a stage knife. A gentleman loaned him a genuine Spanish dirk (not a harmless prop) for theatrical purposes. When the actor got to his penultimate speech—"Bertram hath but one foe on earth, *and he is here*"—he stabbed himself in the heart for real onstage before a horrified audience of Nashville's "beauty and fashion." He was trouper enough to raise himself on an elbow and speak his character's final line: "I died no felon's death—a warrior's weapon freed a warrior's soul!" He died of internal bleeding on March 28 after considerable suffering.

McLaughlin's bizarre stage exit was the subject of much speculation. He knew that the dirk was authentic, so was it suicide? Or had he become so entranced by his role that he said a contemptuous "Fie!" to the consequences of self-stabbing if it gave the audience a thrill? The editor of Nashville's *Western Methodist* newspaper seemed to blame the play's author for creating a character who was just too darn passionate and forceful: "[McLaughlin] became what he represented." The so-called dramatic death was the talk of the nation's press, off and on, for *many* years afterward.

FOLLOW THE BLEEDER

Bonaparte Boyce and a fellow named Powell spent January 5, 1849, shooting the breeze in Dixville, Mercer County. Suddenly, they thought of a great new pastime. The game probably had no official name, but it could be called "Let's see who can take the most throat slashings without dying," and that would get the point across. The winner was to get a quart of whiskey. Powell gave the willing Boyce a few cuts and then severed his jugular vein. Boyce died instantly, so Powell got the whiskey.

BITING THE BISCUIT

Skeptical Mr. Edmonson of McCracken County thought the biscuit baked by his enslaved cook tasted and smelled a little funny. "*You* eat it," he commanded the cook, who did so "very reluctantly" according to a press report. She died of poisoning fifteen minutes later. This occurred on April 24, 1854.

FIREARM CAUTIONARY TALES

On the first of February 1853, in Henderson County, William Green's son put the muzzle of a gun in his mouth and his toe on the trigger "in sport" to show playmates "how he might shoot himself." His foot slipped, and *might* became *did*. Only three months later, young Bland of Greenville, Muhlenberg County, did the very same thing for the very same reason with the very same result.

Target shooting was underway at Knapp's Garden in Louisville on May 1, 1861. As Jacob Ackermann stood in a pit behind the target, he wondered why there had been a delay in the firing. He raised his head in curiosity at exactly the wrong time.

The young gentlemen and belles of Logan County were having a party in early April 1865. One of their less intelligent amusements was snapping an empty pistol at each other. After the group left for dinner, a little boy secretly put a bullet in the gun before they returned, to the extreme misfortune of Olivia Browning once the festivities recommenced.

During Christmas break 1867, a youth put a paper wad in a gun and shot it at a Madison County boy named Davis, all for yux. But the wad hit with sufficient force to kill.

On October 30, 1888, John Williamson, an employee of Copp's stave factory in Daviess County, desired to hunt. Wisely, he wanted to see whether the shotgun was loaded, but his method of determining so left something to be desired. He put his mouth on the muzzle, placed his foot on the hammer, and blew into the barrel. The local paper's sub-headline: "A Man Blows into a Gun to Settle a Doubtful Point and It Is Promptly Settled."

SPEED KILLS!

An extraordinary funeral procession took place in Louisville on Sunday, November 28, 1852. It consisted of fifty-two carriages and fifty mounted horsemen, extending over several city blocks. The guest of honor was John Mooney, a drayman and cartman by trade. Cartmen drove delivery carts, so one might wonder how a man with such a humble job drew a long and extravagant procession. A drayman, however, delivered beer to saloons, so that might explain it. But Mooney is not our focus, rather an accident that occurred while this preposterously long line of mourners trooped back from the cemetery.

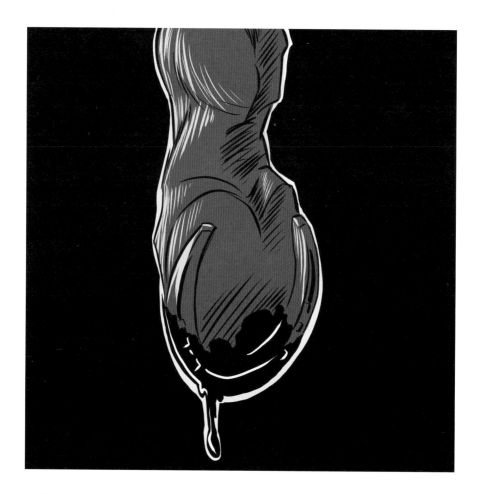

Forty men on horseback rode with reckless speed on Jefferson Street. Their big hurry was never explained. When Dr. J.W. Campbell, a man *not* in the procession, was near Fifteenth Street, he fell off his horse and was trampled. One hoof struck him behind the right ear, effectively crushing his head and killing him nearly instantly. "When taken up, he was a perfect gore of blood, the blood pouring from his ears, mouth, and nostrils in streams," related a reporter. The careless equestrians even hit the poor man's horse so hard that it rolled over twice, just as in a modern car crash.

Although Campbell was run over by several mourners, police settled on one as the specific culprit who destroyed the doctor's head: Martin Ryan, who rode a distinctive black horse. He obviously knew he was guilty, too, since the police found him at home, hiding between two feather mattresses. He had also shaved his beard, for all the good it did.

Ryan was in police court the next day. There was no shortage of witnesses who saw him run into Dr. Campbell's horse, though no one suggested he did it deliberately. At his trial for manslaughter, held on December 13, Ryan was found guilty and sentenced to three years in the penitentiary.

The same week, a guy found guilty of stealing a guitar was sentenced to *four* years in the penitentiary.

AN UNSEEMLY STUNT

Bill Tillman was found drowned in a spring at St. Charles Mines, Hopkins County, on November 16, 1873. The strange part was there was only six inches of water. The stranger part was that Tillman was found standing on his head.

WHAT'S SO FUNNY?

Annie Ayres, a twenty-six-year-old housewife in Covington, Kenton County, spent November 15, 1893, hard at work on domestic chores. She washed and then cooked the evening meal. Something struck her as amusing while she was in the middle of her meal, and she started laughing uncontrollably. Or maybe it was a hysterical reaction to her drudgery. In any case, she laughed so hard and so long that she had to be hospitalized. Doctors said her case would end fatally.

NEWTON'S REVENGE

The town of Franklin once had an elderly Black inventor. Unfortunately, his name is lost to history since the article from the *Franklin Patriot* that details his tragic triumph doesn't mention it, and other back issues don't exist. This inventor claimed to have developed a perpetual motion machine. It was described thusly: "It is a wagon, so arranged that after being set in motion, it runs itself by virtue of the fact that the weight of gravitation is thrown forward of the center of motion and, consequently, the machine is compelled to run."

The Simpson County fair was scheduled for September 9, 1874, and the inventor wanted to show off the device, so on September 2 he climbed aboard, "adjusted the bands, tipped the balance-weight over the center of motion," and steered off for the fairgrounds at a (then) breathtaking speed of fifteen miles an hour.

A mile from home, as the inventor got to the fork of the Cross Plains and Springfield Roads, he tried to steer onto the proper path. The right front wheel struck an oak sapling, pitching the hometown genius overboard. His head struck a fence, and he was killed instantly. The wagon kept going on its own volition until it was blocked by a log. "Since the tragic death of the inventor," said the *Franklin Patriot*, "no man has dared to mount the fiery, untamed steed, but our informant assures us that it will be on exhibition at the fairgrounds, and we invite the attention of inventors and machinists to its peculiar mechanism."

The paper added: "We will not vouch for any man's life who mounts it, but it can be managed safely on the half-mile track on the fairgrounds, and will be put to the best speed, if any man can be found who is competent to guide it." One wonders if there were any takers.

Incidentally, a perpetual motion machine is an impossibility, as it would violate Newtonian physics. I can't explain why, so Google it. But if the description of the machine is accurate, it sounds as though the inventor may have created an early self-propelled vehicle, something like an engineless automobile. That also would have been remarkable.

CARRION, MY WAYWARD SON

A group of Italians worked as section hands for the L&N Railroad at Corbin, Knox County. On the evening of October 21, 1907, one of them killed what seemed a meaty, sizable bird and converted it into stew. He invited three friends to partake. All four became very ill soon, and one ended his earthly activities within a few hours. The tempting fowl was a vulture—or, in their native tongue, *avvoltoio*. In any language: not good eating.

SEE YOU IN HECK

Just before shooting himself on that long-ago July 26, 1902, Samuel Lamb of Louisville said to his wife: "In two minutes I'll be in hell. We won't have any quarrels there." The wording suggested that he fully expected to meet her someday in the same locale.

AN UNWELCOME SURPRISE

In March 1900, Louisville resident Mike Sheehan, who evidently had an alcohol problem, opened a door on the third floor of the house at 523 First Street, thinking the tiny room a convenient place to store a whiskey bottle. He came face to face with John Mobley, who had strangled himself. The body was only a foot away from Sheehan when he pulled the door ajar, so one might easily comprehend his dismay. It must have seemed funny to everyone who wasn't Mike Sheehan, as a local paper made a cynical joke at the finder's expense: "Sheehan got a temperance lecture…that will last him until he can get the price of another drink."

AN UNHEALTHY PUN

James Godman of Harrison County told his wife in February 1875: "I'm going to the smokehouse to hang some of your meat." After he was gone longer than seemed necessary, investigators found that the meat he had in mind was himself.

IRONIC WORDS

Silva Gay of Kentucky was in New Orleans on April 9, 1855. After attending a religious service, she sang, "Oh Lord, take me," and immediately died of apoplexy.

There James Barnett was, just catching tobacco worms on that day in September 1876. "It's a mighty pretty day," said the Hancock County farmer, who dropped dead just after saying so.

THERE MUST BE EASIER WAYS TO ENCOURAGE A DOG TO CHASE A SQUIRREL

Robert Scott, a farmer who lived six miles from Winchester, Clark County, employed an Irishman named Kelly who had a disconcerting foible. He loved nothing more than scrambling up trees and chasing squirrels across the limbs so they would leap to the ground and he could have the incomparable pleasure of watching his dog chase them. One day in September 1855, he was found dying at the foot of a tree and clutching broken twigs, circumstances that told the whole story.

WHAT'S THE RUSH?

Mr. Ash, an Indiana farmer, traveled across the river to Carrollton, Carroll County, on April 4, 1856, and bought a dime's worth of arsenic. He was in such a hurry to climb the Golden Stair and make the coroner earn his taxpayer-funded salary that he swallowed not just the poison but also the paper and twine it was wrapped in.

DO I LOOK LIKE A FLY TO YOU?

Mr. Webster walked into the barroom of a Sharpsburg, Bath County, hotel in June 1856 and ordered a drink. The establishment's owner absentmindedly handed him a bottle of *something* both took to be liquor. It was actually corrosive sublimate—in other words, fly poison. Webster took a slug and harrowed up his soul after an unpleasant week, and indignant locals presumably took their custom elsewhere.

AN UNSOLICITED GIFT

On the night of July 20, 1857, a dead man came floating down the mighty Mississippi at Hickman, Fulton County. The body was secured; a coroner's jury met at the site, examined it, rendered some learned verdict; and everyone in town went to bed happy, assuming the authorities would properly dispose of the waterlogged stranger.

Instead, the salaried public servants left the fellow where he was found for thirty hours (in hottest July), merely tied to the shore with a string. Finally, a sexton named Moxley sauntered along, but instead of giving the body a Christian burial as was his responsibility, he put it in a box and pushed it back into the river to drift away and become some downstream community's problem.

The local paper, the *Hickman Argus*, was not pleased: "We can find no language sufficiently strong in which to express our condemnation of such inhuman conduct. The corpse of a *dog* would not have been treated more carelessly in any decent community. We hope the authorities will look to it; if they do *not*, they shall hear of it again."

LOVEDAY DOES NOT AIM TO PLEASE

Carl Loveday of Louisville was feeling depressed on April 21, 1858, because a young lady in Baltimore had been untrue, and thought he would bid good day to the world forever. He went to Dr. Gunn and asked for a prescription for arsenic "to kill rats." The physician noted well the young man's nervousness and, correctly guessing his real intention, refused to sell it. Loveday made equally unsuccessful attempts to wheedle ratsbane, strychnine or just any old poison—he wasn't particular. Frustrated, Carl said, "I will kill myself before nightfall!" and drew a pistol from his coat pocket.

Dr. Gunn persuaded him to put it away. After Loveday made another failed attempt to buy arsenic, he melodramatically cried, "God bless you, doctor, and God bless my mother!" Then the distraught youth meant to shoot himself, but the gun went off prematurely in his pocket. He escaped with a powder burn and a hole in his trousers, but the bullet plugged Dr. Gunn just above the knee, giving him a painful flesh wound. Loveday offered profuse apologies—not much else he could do. A few minutes later, he was arrested.

Loveday faced police court on April 22. A jury decided he was sane, but perhaps a little silly, and he was dismissed with a stern lecture on the twin follies of leaving this great old world prematurely and shooting bystanders. The jury ruled incorrectly. By May, Loveday was considered a "confirmed lunatic." His brother took him to Baltimore where, on July 17, he shot a

man named John Westervelt. But his aim was off again, and his would-be victim was not seriously injured. "Loveday evidently has the mind to shoot," remarked the *Louisville Courier*, "but fortunately, he don't shoot well."

A whole year later, on October 15, 1859, the *Courier* found humor in Loveday's incompetence when discussing the recent case of a Cincinnati man who aimed a gun at his own head yet missed: "He was almost as bad a marksman as the chap in this city who, a few months ago, drew his pistol and solemnly bidding the world farewell, shot—Dr. Gunn in the leg!"

A THIEF IN THE NIGHT

Late in April 1865, someone broke into Mr. Hunter's house six miles from Bardstown, Nelson County. The burglar took loose change but left a note stating that he would be back in two weeks, and Hunter better have $800 ready for him. On the night of May 12, the Hunter family and neighbors hid with loaded guns, curious to see if the thief would be dumb enough to return as promised. He didn't show, but he did make an appearance the following night along with an equally bright companion. What happened next it is unnecessary to state, except to note that one housebreaker escaped and the other did not.

ON THE HIDDEN DANGERS OF HOG STEALING

Deep in the night of April 7, 1869, Martin Clay of Lexington thought stealing a hog was the thing to do. Rather than just grab it and head for home, he killed and butchered the pig on the spot. He was found dead in Alexander Bradley's field three miles from town next morning with the incriminating meat beside him. There were no marks of violence on his body, and the cause of death was uncertain. The corpse was brought to the Fayette County courthouse, and the meat, and both were put on display for crowds of curiosity seekers to behold. The coroner had a go at the body and determined that Clay had died when a blood vessel ruptured, probably from the strain of carrying that carcass. Some considered Clay's fate "a judgment sent on him for his crime."

51

But that wasn't the end of it. A rumor started that Clay had a seizure and been unconscious for thirty hours. His wife, knowing of his medical condition, allegedly had not buried him. It was said that he had revived and was alive (even after the coroner autopsied him?). A local paper countered, "It is a mistake. Martin is fatally dead and has been buried long ago. The devil didn't warn Martin for nothing."

Speaking of warnings, not everyone took seriously Clay's cautionary tale of things that can go amiss when stealing hogs. Only two weeks after his death, another would-be swine swiper at Nicholasville was killed when he tripped and fell on the hatchet and butcher knife he carried in a sack.

SPORTING EVENTS

It used to be customary to begin sporting events by having an official fire a starting pistol—something we see even now in track races. But wasn't that dangerous? Did anyone ever get killed by a poorly aimed shot? It happened at least once. On September 23, 1927, a former professor at Madison County High School intended to fire a shot to start the second quarter of a football game between the school and Winchester High School. He stood a seemingly safe two hundred feet across the field and aimed straight upward, but the pistol didn't fire. The second time, he inadvertently lowered the gun as he pulled the trigger. The bullet hit fourteen-year-old student Charles Minter in the head. He died a few days later, and the professor was found guilty of involuntary manslaughter and fined $500 on February 16, 1928.

A different kind of unfathomable, fatal accident occurred at Western Kentucky University (then Western State Teachers College) in Bowling Green on April 22, 1935, when an athlete threw a javelin that struck freshman track student Julius Justice in the chest. The student who threw it shouted a warning when he saw where it was heading, but Justice did not hear him.

SNAKE TALES

James Wright of Cincinnati had been living in Vanceburg, Lewis County, for less than a year when a rattlesnake bit his hand on July 4, 1859. A reporter tells us that "the usual remedies were immediately resorted to," probably meaning lots of whiskey, but Wright died that night. This is the weird part: "In preparing the body to be laid out, a singular phenomenon presented itself. There was a picture of the snake itself—perfect in shape and color, and as distinct as if daguerreotyped there—extending from the point on his hand where the fangs had struck, up the arm to the shoulder, and then down to the groin."

Mr. Henry of Greenup County, who was working in Bath County as a miner, considered himself quite the snake charmer and set out to impress pals with his talents on July 30, 1873. He emerged from a mine carrying a gigantic rattler. The assembled miners, mechanics, managers, clerks and bookkeepers could clearly see, even if Henry the self-proclaimed expert couldn't, that the snake was in a foul temper and in no mood to be petted. Henry chortled at their trepidation and made the beginner's mistake of grasping the serpent by the *middle*, giving it the opportunity to double back and chomp its handler's knee. Henry pretended it was no big deal, but he could not keep up the veneer of nonchalance once the swelling set in. He seemed better after imbibing a quart of whiskey. Records don't reveal whether Henry survived his adventure, but assuredly no good came of it.

SILENT SUICIDE

On January 24, 1864, a Mr. Nolin elected to die by suicide at the Daviess County home of Robert Campbell. He got in bed, pulled the covers over his head and cut his own throat. He did it so subtly that none of the several other persons in the room knew about it, not even a man sitting on the bed.

ASSUME NOTHING

Steaven A. Jones of Murray, Calloway County, was crushed by a collapsing tree on February 12, 1871. He heard the creaking and snapping sound of it falling but assumed a neighbor was making noises to scare him.

DEATH BY FRUIT

Everybody in the old times knew that if you ate too much fruit you would likely catch cholera, so Englishman Charles Walker, living in Maysville, Mason County, thought he could kill himself if he overindulged in green apples. He added generous portions of bologna, milk crackers and whiskey to the menu. He died the next day, July 18, 1873. Perhaps the whiskey got him or indigestion from his unseemly meal. Or perhaps he did expire from the cholera he foolhardily invited. People in 1873 didn't realize that the fruit didn't cause the fatal disease but rather the fecal germs left on it through poor sanitation.

5

MY OLD KENTUCKY (HAUNTED) HOME

Numinous Noises

At least two previous tenants, Mr. Waddell and Mr. M.W. Matthews, had lived in the Hickman County house. Mr. Rison was dwelling there in early 1873, but evidently something else was as well. The hauntings manifested chiefly as unaccountable noises. Sometimes Rison—described as a "calm, sensible, reflecting man" who did not believe in spirits—heard bare feet walking. At other times it sounded like a fight, or doors opening and shutting or tumbling furniture. Usually, though not always, the sounds issued from the unused upper floor, and they were heard by all family members, hired help and former residents. The noises came night and day but normally at night. Rison assured skeptics that he had checked many times and never could find the sounds' source. But once while searching he found human bones hidden in the attic, left there by a former lodger who thought they made interesting home décor. Mr. Rison did not believe there was a connection between the remains and the racket, but you might beg to differ.

Sulking in His Room

Twenty-four-year-old Richard Bland Ballard of Ballard neighborhood, Nelson County, planned to marry a Miss Rhodes on December 31, 1872. His father, Thomas H. Ballard, opposed the match and was angered that he

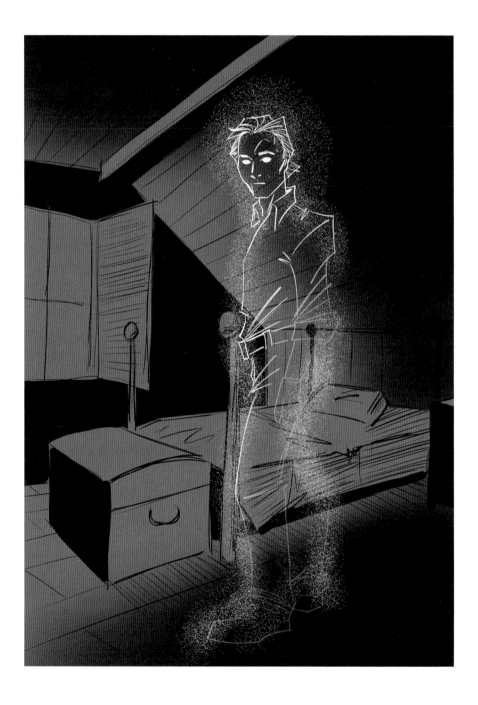

was informed about the nuptials at the last minute. On Friday, December 13, Bland asked his father what he thought of the bride-to-be, and Thomas answered, "I think the girl will get the worst of it."

"I wish I were dead," snarled Bland, who turned word into deed by going outside and shooting himself. On December 17, searchers Milt and Drury Bryan found his body lying in a forest pathway, still guarded by his dog. He was buried in Holy Cross Cemetery in Marion County.

But Bland refused to rest in his suicide's grave. In early March 1873, it was reported that his spirit made regular trips to the old homestead. Most ghosts have their own inner glow, a lovely thing to behold, but Bland carried a light. Witnesses said the ghost would open the front door at night and walk in just as though he still lived in the place, trudge to his old bedroom like a truculent teenager and rummage through his trunks in search of who knows what, because nobody dared ask. At least once Ballard spoke to his son's shade but received no reply. Soon after, Bland's sister entered his room and saw him rising from the floor by his open trunk. Interestingly, the last thing Bland did on earth before rushing out to kill himself was search his trunk, as witnessed by his sister.

There were multiple witnesses: Bland's father, brother and sister all swore his ghost appeared nightly and behaved as described. A tall tale, perhaps, but one would-be explanation was even taller: some theorized that a man who wanted to buy the farm impersonated the ghost to scare Mr. B into selling it. The press does not tell us when, or if, Bland ceased his home visits, so perhaps he found what he was searching for in his belongings and afterward merely pouted in his casket.

VANISHING VANDAL

As of 1883, it was still visible by the roadside on a high bank of the Licking River just off North Main Street in West Liberty, Morgan County: a mound with a stone at each end, obviously a grave, but with no identifying inscriptions. It was the final resting place of Morris Hagerty (or Haggerty) of Cincinnati, a murdered Irish peddler of tablecloths. (Most sources say the murder occurred in 1855, but through the magic of backbreaking research we find that it was in early January 1853.) William H. Brown was hanged for the crime on December 9, 1853.

Hagerty's grave had a feature that stood out. People claimed to see mysterious lights and hear muffled voices there. One farfetched story maintained that Hagerty's spirit entered Dr. Thornley's house, lifted the doctor's knife from his pocket and broke his queensware. Locals took the ghost seriously enough that at least one real estate transaction in the area was canceled when the potential buyer had second thoughts.

In any case, Hagerty still haunts West Liberty in another fashion. Peddler Street is named for him, and at the end of the street he lies entombed in a grave cut in a rock, according to a 1977 account by Helen Price Stacy. As for his killer, Brown, he reposes under a common stone in the Brown Cemetery at Rockhouse. The spot where he was hanged is, or was, "low on a hillside at the end of a short hollow just off Prestonsburg Street." The hanging tree long ago turned white and died.

A DISRUPTED HONEYMOON

In the late nineteenth century, there was a house near Petersburg, Boone County, that passersby avoided if possible. The story went that early in the county's history, the two-story frame structure was the residence of a newlywed couple. A few weeks after the wedding, they were murdered. A jilted rival was suspected, but he fled and presumably was never found.

The house's chronicler reported that it was seldom tenanted for long; in fact, most occupancies could be measured in hours. One man moved in and moved right back out the next morning. He admitted that he saw nothing out of the ordinary, but the sounds of footfalls and a struggle "took the starch completely out of him."

The man's hasty departure was followed by a succession of scoffers who packed their bags and took up residence only to vacate with haste, generally on the next day. Finally, the house's owner vowed to give it, along with five acres, to whomever could live there for one year. The offer caught the ear of a brave man who moved his furniture into the house one afternoon. By dawn, he and his belongings were outta there.

At long last, a group of Petersburg smarties determined to stay overnight by occupying various parts of the house in groups of two. As usual, they saw nothing but heard plenty. The well-established sounds of a fight started out faintly and appeared to move from room to room if the gentlemen got too close. Their bravery correspondingly shrank as the noises increased, and before long they sought quiet, non-haunted locations in town.

The community was so afraid of the house that some talked of burning it down so they could be rid of it. But someone pointed out—on what authority I do not know—that if an arsonist set fire to the abode, the ghost(s) would only take up residence with him instead. As of 1891, the crumbling house still stood, a haven for bats only. Presumably, time and the elements have obliterated it, leaving one to wonder where its ghosts went.

THE FRIGHTENER AND THE FRIGHTENED

The old house stood near Tygart Creek, twelve miles from Greenup. An elderly couple named Hyers lived there first. One night, Mr. Hyers died unexpectedly. His wife said it was cholera; an examination proved he had been poisoned. But by the time this discovery was made, she had long since fled.

Several months later, a family from Magoffin County named Musgrove moved in despite the house's haunted reputation. On the night of June 21, 1895, while Mr. Musgrove was staying overnight elsewhere on business, his wife was awakened by agonized groans. As she sought the source, Mr. Hyers strolled by the front window as though he still owned the place. The lady of the house grabbed her two children and ran away.

Word traveled fast, and neighborhood men spent the rest of that night of June 21 in the old Hyers house. Twice more the former tenant passed the front window. The investigators approached him once, and another time, they fired at him. Both times he vanished with a contemptuous ease that makes envious living people wish they were ghosts too.

However, the story may have ended fatally for Mrs. Musgrove, who was so frightened by her encounter that some doubted she would recover. It may be that the old site now has two ghosts, the frightener and the frightened.

GHOST PRISONERS

Burrill Bush, a Black lunatic, died in the Clark County jail in the spring of 1868. In mid-April, a prisoner said that he was awakened by a voice calling his name. When he opened his eyes, he saw that the cell door was open. But he did not avail himself of the chance to escape, possibly because a ghost was standing there. It was "a large-framed Negro, with whiskers on his lower jaw, and wearing a blue overcoat." The ghost said he was concerned about some land he had rented. When the prisoner asked the apparition's name, it vanished and the cell door closed. The inmate provided his keepers with a description that matched Burrill Bush to a tee—interesting, because the prisoner had never met or seen him.

The old Louisville jail was reportedly haunted as far back as 1895. On the night of October 2, turnkey Alf Davis was making his rounds outside the building when he saw a shadow on the rear wall and realized with a start that it wasn't his. Naturally, he thought someone was standing in the yard, but he saw no one. While Alf was contemplating that, he heard what sounded like someone running. No one was visible, and then the shadow disappeared. If there was a ghost, whose was it? A prime candidate might be Charles Dilger, who was very incompetently hanged on the premises in 1889 for killing two policemen. On the night of November 12, 1898, three jail employees heard prisoner Will Lee shrieking and trying to escape. He told them that Dilger had threatened to cut his throat—I suppose with a ghost-knife. He was so distraught that the officials allowed him to sit in the corridor until they could find another cell. Lee assured them he would rather die than again encounter Dilger.

VIBRATING BED, NO DIMES REQUIRED

In November 1894, Sallie Morton, African American owner of a brothel at 826 Grayson Street in Louisville, found salt sprinkled in her yard by next-door neighbor/enemy Alice Tucker. Superstition held that this act would hasten death for the homeowner. The situation was worsened when Morton discovered a red flannel bundle in her bed containing human hair and three fingers severed from a corpse. One imagines Alice did that too. Morton died of angina pectoris on January 18, 1895.

The coroner fulfilled his official responsibilities, after which people carried the body upstairs for burial preparations. The parlor piano began playing "four pieces of mournful music" by itself. Witnesses swore the keys moved though no one was within a foot of the instrument. Just before midnight, according to those present, the bed on which Morton lay started shaking— the very bed that so recently had ensconced three dead fingers. Then the entire room did the same, until "a glass of water could not be kept on the dresser or mattress without a weight being placed on it." Not just for a few seconds, either, but for the entire day of January 19. Two women fainted from fear, and when word got out, a crowd of up to 1,500 gathered in the yard. Police investigated and claimed the water and bed trembled because the floor was shaky, but if that simple explanation were the case, why did no one notice it before?

The funeral was held right there in the brothel on January 20. No preacher showed up, and the crowd—who paid a fellow named "Slippery Bill" ten cents a head for the privilege—gazed with wonder and terror at the body on the still-shaking bed. Bill collected an estimated ten dollars before the cops chased him off. Even after Sallie was buried, the presumably now-penitent Alice Tucker called the police three times on the night of January 27 to check out weird sounds issuing from the vacant house. Some persons who lived in the vicinity were so frightened that they vowed to move from the neighborhood.

The house maintained its reputation nearly a decade later. In September 1904, it was reportedly still untenanted and avoided at all costs to the financial detriment of the owner.

GREATLY ANNOYED

On the night of January 9, 1874, forty impatient men went to the jail in Greenville, Muhlenberg County, and forced the jailer to release prisoner Dudley White, accused shooter of John Gosett (or Gossett). They hanged White from a tree behind a cemetery.

That would usually be the end of the story, but perhaps not in this case. In early February, two young men reportedly rode by White's house when the ghost of the hanged man stepped out of the yard "looking as natural as life" and kept unwanted company with them for some distance, sometimes walking *around* their horses and sometimes *under* them, singular behavior even for a ghost. On their return trip, White came back and performed the same actions.

White, it appears, haunted not only his own house but also someone else's: "When the Negro was found hanging to a limb the day after his execution, he was taken down and 'laid out' in an old house nearby. It is said that he is now often seen at this house, passing up and down stairs and moving about in a mysterious and restless manner."

But there's more! A Mr. Youts, "one of the most reliable and respectable men in the neighborhood," often saw the shade of Gosett pacing near the spot where he was murdered. Mr. Youts was reportedly "greatly annoyed."

UNREAL ESTATE

It's a fact: some houses attain a bad reputation from dark deeds that occurred within them, inspiring rumors that the joint is haunted. In 2003, the Kentucky legislature passed a "stigmatized properties" law (KRS 324.162, if you want to look it up). According to Lee B. Harris, the new law stated that real estate agents "do not have to disclose anything about a property that is not specifically required to be disclosed by state or federal law....Licensees are not required to disclose murders, suicides, or ghosts in a property, for example." Before then, sellers "were required to assess whether a property was stigmatized on a case-by-case basis to determine if a failure to disclose a particular stigma would be a violation of...the statute that mandates disclosure of any known defects."

In other words, before 2003, agents could freely choose whether to tell you about the massacre that happened in the living room, and now they don't have to tell you at all. You will be forewarned about leaking pipes or roof damage, but not about revenants of the restless dead reportedly lurking in the attic.

It has always been a problem for those who rent or sell dwellings. How much about the house's unsavory past does the potential buyer need to know? *If I sell the place and the owner claims after the fact that it is haunted—like those folks in Amityville, New York, did back in the '70s—what sort of legal problems may ensue?* As far back as 1905, a Louisville real estate agent complained that his lot in life was made harder by "superstitious" White and Black prospective tenants who refused to rent homes they thought were haunted:

> *A lot of people think the day of the ghost is past, but anyone in my business knows that spooks are still plentiful and vigorous. I know of a dozen houses right here in Louisville where ghosts have full sway and are never disturbed for more than one night at a time* [because tenants would move in and move back out so quickly, that is]. *You have no idea how many people refuse to live in houses that are haunted.*

The agent implied that the "ghosts" were all caused by squeaky stairs, creaky boards, loose flues and the like and that a handyman could exorcise the spirits for good. Which begs the question: if that was the problem, why didn't he hire a carpenter to fix the houses and make them sellable?

WHAT DID STARR SEE?

Mr. Starr of Southville, Shelby County, got up early to plow one morning in July 1876. As he worked, he was surprised to see a man walking among his wheat shocks. Starr thought it must be a neighbor—but why did the man make a point of keeping his back turned? When the farmer made it to the end of his field, he turned his team of horses to plow in the opposite direction and saw that the man was still traipsing wordlessly around in his field. When Starr got close enough to get a clear look at the figure, it took three long strides, raised its arms to the sky, levitated just above the ground, traveled twenty feet and vanished, presumably never to be seen again. The newspaper correspondent who related the weird sighting remarked, "[Starr] is neither superstitious nor timid…and of undoubted courage and coolness. [He] will convince anyone who will talk to him of his own honest belief in the apparition. On one or two occasions he was within twenty feet of it, and it could not possibly have been an optical illusion."

A HUSBAND FROM (PRESUMABLY) HELL

Eliza Green's husband, Richard, died of a long illness at their home in Washington County on March 18, 1874. Three months later, things started happening. The widow Green heard noises night and day that sounded like someone miserably ill or thrashing about in pain. And then, said the *Springfield Kentuckian*, "[S]he saw frequently in her room at night after the lamp was lighted, a shadowy figure resembling the head and shoulders of a medium-sized man moving around the wall next [to] the ceiling and uniformly as the shadow reached the lamp the flame was extinguished, and this phenomenon happened as often as four or five times in the night." Sometimes she heard clear footsteps in her room but could see no one, even with the lamp burning. Once, a gauzy white form half-filled the back door of her bedroom. She fled the house. Mrs. Green had witnesses to some of these phenomena; for example, in the presence of visitors, the front door opened violently and slammed shut with such force flowerboxes fell out of the windows.

The ghost's last appearance was on June 30. As Mrs. Green gathered kindling wood in the cellar, she saw a man's lower legs and feet standing nearby and then felt the touch of a cold hand on her shoulder. She looked up, and there was Mr. White in his burial clothes.

Her calm eloquence on this occasion is to be admired: "In the name of the Lord Jesus Christ who redeemed me, Dick, what do you want?" He told her, in his natural tone of voice, of the torments that await the unsaved and dropped a disturbing hint that she was among this category. He came back "to advise her of her neglect of duty, and to urge her to act otherwise." He had imperative messages for three local persons—his brother Charles Green, Rachel Walker and a Miss Edgerton—which implies they had good cause to be worried, too, and let us hope they took the warning. He further asked that masses be said for his soul. Then he said "friend" three times and disappeared.

After that morning, Mrs. Green sometimes heard groaning and knocking on the floor, but at least she saw no further manifestations.

RAPPER'S DELIGHT

In 1855, a family named Parks lived on Madison Street in Newport, Campbell County. Strange noises in the night such as rappings on the walls and thumps on the floor, and the furniture's rearranging itself,

convinced them that they shared their abode with remnants of the hostile dead. Around the third week of June, Mr. Parks awoke feeling dreadfully thirsty, but as the nocturnal noises were resounding through the house, he expressed a fear of getting up for a drink.

Mrs. Parks angrily retorted, "In the name of the devil, if you want to drink go and get it. The devil will protect you from the ghosts!"

Whether Parks was most afraid of the ghost, the devil or his temperamental wife we cannot say. But he got out of bed, maybe as the rappings resounded about him (because that makes a better story). He fell downstairs and broke his neck. His horrified family found him dead at the foot of the stairs.

Now, skeptics might say that venturing downstairs in the dark is a risky proposition in any case. But the Parks family believed the ghost killed the paterfamilias and were so alarmed that they buried him in secret without alerting the coroner. They moved to an undisclosed location as quickly as possible. The only reason the story got out at all was that an elderly peddler woman saw Mr. Parks's body before it was buried. If the residence had no ghost before, perhaps it did after.

HEADLESS IN HARRODSBURG

Strange doings appear to have been afoot in Mercer County in August 1874. On their way home from Richmond one night in August, Robert Gallagher and J.C. Ewing passed the fence at former governor Magoffin's residence. They saw a headless man in the road. Their buggy passed over it, but when they investigated, the decapitated one was gone. Others saw it on later occasions, but the specter hasn't been seen in many a moon. Perhaps, despite its headless condition, it had the good sense to go wherever it was going rather than stick around in the highway.

SPIRIT AND SPIRITS

Mike Callahan thought he saw a ghost on Lafayette Street in Louisville in 1868 and got so scared that he got drunk, and remained so in perpetuity. As of September 1870, he was reportedly still inebriated.

PEST, PEST, PERTURBED SPIRIT

On May 2, 1870, John Morton shot and killed Daniel Powers in a house of ill fame on Louisville's Eleventh Street, run by Annie Rayburn (or Rabourne). Their quarrel was over a woman named Carrie Dean. Mrs. Rayburn was evicted after the bad publicity and set up business in a new location, 205 Lafayette Street. On August 12, Daniel's brother Albert came to the brothel and shot Mrs. Rayburn with a pistol he had pawned his coat to buy, seriously wounding her.

Inquiring minds wanted to know why Powers shot Mrs. Rayburn. He replied that the ghost of his brother had given the command. According to Albert, Daniel came to his bedside one night and told him, "Al, I want you to go and kill that woman for me; it is impossible for me to do it." Albert agreed, but the next morning assumed it was all just a dream and did nothing, because no dream was going to tell him what to do.

But Dan's shade returned a week later and made rather a pest of himself on the subject: "[H]e came again and asked me why I had not done as he asked me. I replied that I could not realize that he had been to see me, and thought it was all a dream. He then told me that, if I loved him as a brother, he wanted me to go and kill that woman, and he insisted that I should do it." The next day Albert tried to procure a gun but couldn't and was secretly relieved, as he really didn't want to shoot Mrs. Rayburn. Dan was out of ghostly patience on his third visit, telling his reluctant sibling, "Al, if you don't go and kill that woman, I will kill *you*." Albert protested that he didn't have the money to buy a weapon. "Hock your coat," argued Dan, which, as related, is exactly what Al did. After he shot Mrs. Rayburn, the satisfied ghost stopped bothering him.

Did the police believe the novel blame-the-ghost defense? Apparently not, as Al was clapped in jail on $3,000 bond and the grand jury indicted him on September 5.

6

PROGNOSTICATED PASSINGS

Sometimes the Death Angel gives a shout-out ahead of time. Take the case of Cornelius "Niece" Turner, a Warren County politician who served in the Kentucky House from 1816 to 1820 before being elected to the state senate. In 1822, a disembodied voice told him that he would die at a certain time on a certain day. Turner believed the information wholeheartedly. One might think that such knowledge would make the hearer a nervous wreck, living constantly in dread of the coming time and ticking off each passing day with fear, but Turner was made of sterner stuff. He took the prediction with equanimity. Indeed, thinking that he had a known expiration date only focused his energies on tasks to be performed. In 1835, Turner took ill at about age sixty. His kin told the long-standing family story to an attending doctor and added that if the voice were correct, Turner would pass away in ten days. The physician didn't believe a word of it—until Turner died at exactly the predicted time on August 22, 1835. Forty years later, the unnamed but "eminent" Bowling Green doctor confirmed the story to a reporter for the local paper.

Mrs. Montague was sitting by the fireside at her home in Newport, Campbell County, one morning in January 1850 when she nonplussed her family by suddenly rising and saying, "Go get the neighbors. I want them to come and see me die." She seemed in good health, but her relatives humored her and brought them in. As the group watched, she died in her bed. It is not recorded exactly why Mrs. Montague wanted to entertain the neighbors thus.

Clara Jacques of Louisville came down with cholera on July 23, 1850. Dr. Knight made a house call and provided her husband, grocer Henry Jacques, with a grim diagnosis: her case was terminal. The husband calmly handed his watch to his brother and said, "My wife is going to die, and I cannot live without her. I shall die too." Though he seemed healthy, that's exactly what he did three hours later. They were buried in Western Cemetery, but their gravestones bear the erroneous death date of August 24.

Rebecca Air, an inmate of the poorhouse at Newport, died at age seventy-four on December 18, 1865, but not before giving away her few worldly goods to friends since she said she would need them no longer. Though seemingly in good health, she underwent a violent fit of paralysis and died. For years, she had been convinced that she would have a presentiment when the Pale Rider was cantering in her direction.

In mid-July 1869, an unnamed Marion County man told coworkers he would die at 4:00 p.m. the next day. He told them again the next morning, no doubt to their merriment. But at precisely the stroke of four o'clock, he became an object of interest to the coroner, the undertaker and very likely, the medical student and the grave robber. The deceased had also predicted that a storm of unprecedented fury would strike the region on August 7, but that prognostication was a fizzle.

George Hoblitzel of Louisville astounded his family at lunchtime on June 30, 1870, by saying, "I will not live longer than five more minutes." His wife ignored the remark, since he seemed in good health. True to his word, ere five minutes passed Hoblitzel was dead of apoplexy (a stroke).

Sixteen-year-old Sam Miller of Big Reedy, Edmonson County, died after a brief illness on December 24, 1870. Several weeks after this tragic event, his father, John, found the following inscription in Samuel's penmanship in his account book, written twelve days before he died: "Samuel M. Miller is my name and single is my life. I am going to die on the 24th day of December, 1870. I hate to leave all of my friends and connections. Good-bye to all my friends."

Mary Walker Bell, wife of Captain Darwin Bell of Christian County, died on December 27, 1872. She had predicted the date and time of her passing several weeks before. "Mrs. Bell was said to be a lady of rare gifts," said her obituary, and one of them was premortem prophecy.

A few hours before his death on Friday, February 27, 1874, Jacob VanMeter of Warren County said something along these lines: "Better make my grave extra large, because my wife will die immediately after me." No one was alarmed, since Martha VanMeter was in good health. But the next

day she took ill, and she died on Sunday. On Monday, March 2, she joined her husband in Fairview Cemetery.

The night of June 11, 1874: school exercises were taking place at Professor Arnold's Seminary in Oakland, Warren County. An oil lamp on a piano exploded, setting fifteen-year-old Sallie E. Smith's dress on fire as she read a composition called "Tomorrow," resulting in fatal burns. Exactly what her speech was about, the press does not tell us—surely it was not about her dress catching fire—but a reporter noted that it "foretold her own fate as if forewarned."

Young Robert Larkin of Henderson was thrown from a train and killed in mid-October 1874. The day before, Larkin—who had a good vocabulary—had told his father about a disturbing, prophetic dream: "I dreamt this morning I was fireman on a train southward bound, when we were run into by another train and our engine knocked over a steep declivity. I felt myself falling downward, downward, when I awoke. I can't imagine what presentiment has seized me, but I am not at all myself this morning and fear something serious is going to happen."

One night in November 1875, George Murphy of Casey County dreamed that he was killed when his team of horses ran away. He told his family the next morning at breakfast. His wife begged him not to use the team that day, but he replied that he didn't believe in dreams and went to work. By sundown, Mr. Murphy believed in the prognosticative power of dreams, and so did everyone else.

Almanza Byrd of Owingsville, Bath County, spoiled the fine spring morning of April 4, 1908, by bursting into the family room and telling his wife that he had heard a voice saying, "Byrd, you will die before twelve o'clock today." The more she tried to convince him that it was a bunch of nonsense, the more vehement and agitated Almanza became. Finally, at the point of exhaustion, he lay down and died "almost without a struggle." Perhaps the excitement of the argument finished him off?

A.A. Garretson, a carpenter in Russellville, Logan County, was nicknamed "Shakespeare" because he knew the Bard's works so well. After he developed a stomach disease, he expressed a wish that he might die when he turned seventy-two. His fondest desire was fulfilled on his seventy-second birthday, April 26, 1908, when he shuffled off this mortal coil and entered the undiscovered country from whose bourn no traveler returns.

William T. Armstrong of Ballard County predicted that he would die exactly four years after his wife. On September 27, 1909, he did just what he said, dying of "general debility" at age eighty-six.

Engineer William L. Kash of Lexington died on January 11, 1911, when his train exploded near Bagdad, Shelby County, en route to Louisville. Just before taking off, he had told his colleagues: "I've had two bad accidents, and if we have one this run, I guess it will be my last one."

Then there are cases in which precise details or dates of death are predicted not by the soon-to-be-deceased but by someone else, a circumstance no less disturbing. For example, young Ellie Stewart of Knox County dreamed on January 13, 1874, that her father had died in his shop. She told her sister afterward, so there was a witness. Two days later, she entered the shop and found him dead on the floor from heart disease.

One evening in 1908, Winnifred Decker of 622 East Market Street, Louisville, had a nightmare in which her son Arthur, a navy cook, got out of bed dressed in his sailor's uniform. He wandered the streets of a nameless city until he made his way onto a railroad track. A series of cars backed up and accidentally crushed him. The dream then showed a long line of men in military garb following an American flag-draped casket on a carriage. They placed flowers on the casket as it was lowered in the grave. The final act depicted Mrs. Decker receiving letters of condolence from members of the Navy Department. The unpleasant dream became more so when she had it again a few nights later. It bothered her so much, although she thought psychic visions were "all bosh," that she sent Arthur a letter beseeching him to be cautious. Several months later, on September 4, Mrs. Decker received a navy cablegram regretfully informing her that Arthur had been killed by a backing train in Melbourne, Australia, two days earlier. Mrs. Decker died on January 30, 1932, and is buried in Louisville, far from the son she prophetically dreamed about.

Early in the morning of March 24, 1934, twenty-year-old Agnes Brandenburg of Beattyville, Lee County, awoke from a nightmare in which she saw her father, Thomas Brandenburg, drowning in Silver Creek. Later in the morning, her brother found Mr. Brandenburg's car submerged in the creek. Agnes told her family about the dream before the body was found, so it wasn't an after-the-fact prediction.

7

MORBID MISCELLANY

Selling Your Body

A Maysville, Mason County doctor reportedly owned a skeleton in 1873, the original owner of which had swapped the rights to it for a quart of whiskey.

A Pimped-Out Ride

The J.D. Pearson undertaking firm in Louisville purchased a hearse in early 1873 that was considered such a marvel it was featured in a news article deeming it "the finest thing in the way of a funereal turn-out that we have ever seen." Indeed, the description makes it sound as though it would almost have been a *pleasure* to require its services. It had a full clarence front, meaning it was a horse-drawn carriage with room for four passengers in an enclosed cabin and an outer elevated seat for the driver, just the sort of conveyance you'd expect a Disney princess to ride in (but without a black armband and a casket). It had all iron running gear, bullion-fringed inner curtains and gold mountings, which included a pair of lamps for nighttime jaunts to the cemetery. It even won a prize at a Cincinnati exhibition! The splendid, yet depressing, vehicle cost $3,500, which translates to over $70,000 in modern currency, and no doubt many a grieving widow spent years paying off its temporary use when a crape-decorated oxcart would have answered the purpose just as well.

GRAVEYARD DOG

"He was not a pretty dog by any means," mused a local reporter. "He was yellow, shaggy, with a bearded face, cropped ears, [and] a short tail." The public dubbed the dog Bulger. He would have been a study for Pavlov. One day he followed his master's funeral procession from the countryside to Lexington Cemetery. For many years afterward, Bulger lived in the city but followed every passing funeral cortege to the graveyard. The poor creature thought that his owner would be restored to him. After a funeral he would return to the city, wearing what some swore was a weary, disappointed look. Sometimes he wandered the cemetery grounds, "not sportively, but in a melancholy mood," as though aware his master was around there somewhere.

Sympathetic policemen and citizens fed Bulger, but he never allowed himself to be adopted. He and his master were reunited—let us hope so—when the dog passed away in April 1880. "Truly, more genuine constancy has seldom if ever been witnessed," reflected the reporter, and "such love could hardly be deserved."

COFFIN IN PUBLIC

First, the *Louisville Courier-Journal's* Boyle County correspondent boasted about Danville's "institutions of learning," "refined society," "beautiful women," "brave men" and "the sterling integrity of her inhabitants." But then he got around to admitting that at least one unknown denizen sorely lacked respect for private property. A Danville man had acquired several unused coffins, one adult-sized and several smaller ones. The writer noted that they weren't exactly top of the line, having neither silver handles nor satin linings. Yet one night in late February 1873, a thief stole one—and, said the writer, who was clearly disappointed in his fellow man, it was the best in the bunch.

THE HARRODSBURG NEEDLE RAIN REDUX

This story's subject matter doesn't really fit in this book, but that never stopped me before. Readers of *Forgotten Tales of Kentucky* (Arcadia Publishing/ The History Press, 2008) will remember the bizarre story of the rain of knitting needles that Harrodsburg, Mercer County, experienced once upon a time. Here are updates:

Supposedly, the event occurred in March 1856, which I was unable to confirm despite scrutinizing newspapers from that entire year. I found that the basis for the alleged date was a *Ripley's Believe It or Not* cartoon—not generally the most trustworthy of sources—from May 1939. But an 1873 newspaper article in the *Harrodsburg People* dated the event to "about twenty years ago" (circa 1853), and an 1876 article claimed it was "about 1845." The *People* item stated, "If it was a joke, the jokist died with the secret unrevealed."

Taking the sources in aggregate, these facts emerge: the needle rain fell on a hemp factory lot owned by a Mr. Curry (by 1939, it was the site of the Lee Smock Lumber Company); the shower happened during a violent nighttime storm; hundreds of needles of varying sizes fell and were implanted at the same angle; there was no knitting needle factory anywhere nearby, so sayonara to the handy tornado explanation; and citizens owned some of the needles for years afterward. In short, the event appears to be authentic, though the date is still uncertain.

FRIGHTENED? I WAS PETRIFIED

Generally, one loses weight (and plenty of it) after death. But there were people who did just the reverse. A woman living in Nelson County, Virginia, died in 1849. She was originally from Woodford County, Kentucky, and made a dying request to be buried back home. In December 1853, the widower had her exhumed to fulfill her desire. To everyone's surprise, the body of the 110-pound woman seemed to have petrified into a substance resembling limestone while underground. The corpse was so heavy that when taken to the train depot for shipping to Kentucky, it was found to weigh 500 pounds. The widower had to pay corresponding freight charges, and the coffin accounted for an additional 50 pounds, making gratifying the wish an expensive proposition.

After Joseph Black of Barren County died circa 1863, he was buried in a metallic coffin on his farm five miles from the road to Cave City. In early 1883, he was exhumed for reburial in Odd Fellows Cemetery. When the lid was opened, Black turned out to be an odd fellow indeed: he was in perfect, nay, *petrified* condition, his features easily recognizable to old friends. Even his burial clothes were immaculate. But his body weighed a lot more than anyone expected.

The child of George Byers, engineer at the *Owensboro Examiner* newspaper office, died in the summer of 1875. In August 1876, Mr. Byers had the grave opened so he could rebury the child in Elmwood Cemetery. Not only had its face turned to "marble," but the stems of flowers placed in its hands had grown to "considerable length."

The gravediggers were baffled in November 1876 as they tried to pull up the coffin of Jennie Walker Rion, wife of Newton B. Rion Jr., in Paris Cemetery, Bourbon County, who was being moved to another section of the graveyard. She had died ten years before, on October 4, 1866, and everyone remembered her as being slight, weighing probably less than one hundred pounds. But it required six men with ropes to extricate the casket. When they opened the lid, they found that she had "petrified"—all but her nose, which was missing—accounting for her postmortem weight gain.

A woman who died in the Deep South in 1853 was packed in salt as a preservative and sent to her home in Boone County, Kentucky, for burial. Soon afterward, her daughter died and was placed in the same grave. In November 1869, they were exhumed for reburial in Highland Cemetery in Fort Mitchell, Kenton County, and found to be in such superb condition onlookers thought they were petrified.

There once lived in Campbell County a tiny woman named Rachel, no last name given, who many were convinced was a witch. Her reputation was sealed many years after her death when the seventy-pound body was removed from her grave and it required four brawny men to lift her coffin. After it was placed in a wagon, two strong horses strained to move and then gave up. Two more horses were hitched to the team, and even then they barely made it to the newly dug resting place. The 1871 account of this singular event does not mention whether anyone opened the coffin to peer at Rachel—maybe they were afraid to—but if the story is true, it's not difficult to guess the cause of the heaviness: petrifaction!

Eleven family members, all tuberculosis victims who died between 1851 and 1863, were removed from the Portland Avenue graveyard in Louisville in June 1872. The bodies' condition was about as unpromising as one might expect, except one whose skull had turned to rock as hard as Curly's head when Moe bent an iron bar over it.

So what the deuce was going on here? Did the loved and lost really turn to stone by some mysterious procedure? No, it was a disgusting natural process called adiopocere, in which fatty tissue turns to a soaplike substance, especially if submerged in water over a long period of time— e.g., in a leaky casket.

AN UNDIGNIFIED CREMATION

The White mansion at the southwest corner of Seventeenth and Broadway, Louisville, had a reputation for being haunted. For ten years, it was abandoned, then demolished. The American Tobacco Company was built on the site.

On March 5, 1898, workmen were digging on what was once the mansion's yard when they uncovered the skeletons of a child and a woman. She was well-dressed, including high-heeled slippers. The bones crumbled to dust when touched.

Discovering bodies where they are not expected is interesting enough, but a few details made this find extra intriguing. No one could remember there ever having been a cemetery on the location; the body of the woman, at least, was "tightly cemented" in a brick tomb; and most strikingly, they were *headless*. This suggests a murderer who beheaded the corpses to make them difficult to identify if found—yet conversely, who cared enough to dress the woman finely and place her in a tomb rather than simply bury her (and the child) in the forest.

The workers gathered what they could of the bodies and cremated them in the factory's furnace. If the place wasn't haunted before, it should have been after that.

A Pine-Scented Air Freshener Needed, or Body Odor Problem

Mary Snyder died at her home on Seventeenth Street, Louisville, on June 15, 1894. The wake was held the next night at the home of the deceased, as was custom at the time. Mrs. Snyder's body was decomposing with gusto, as her family was too poor to afford a first-rate embalming and it was steamy summertime. The odor was so powerful that most mourners remained in the yard. Undertaker Bax did not attend in person, but to prevent a general pestilence even though it would have increased his business, he provided Snyder's family with a disinfectant cloth to place over the corpse's mouth and a bottle of disinfectant liquid to pour on the cloth. Bax warned everyone to handle the fluid carefully, as it was a deadly poison.

Mattie Burns (age fourteen), Della Farris (also fourteen) and Lizzie Moran (sixteen) remained inside as Good Samaritans. Every so often, they poured more of that powerful poison on the cloth covering Mrs. Snyder's mouth. Before long, they began reeling about the place. Della fainted, landing face-first. Mattie and Lizzie bolted outside and sagged against a fence. They all had to be carried home.

One gossipy neighbor whispered that they had gotten drunk at the wake, also a custom at the time. In fact, there was whiskey in the house, but the girls' indignant parents insisted that the reek issuing from the late Mrs. Snyder and her mouth-rag made them sick. If so, that was one epic stink! Check out the aftereffects: "Since then all three of the girls have been in a very precarious position. At times they rave as if they were insane; at others, they are totally unconscious, and the seeming fits are almost without cessation. During these fits the arms, legs, and head work convulsively and rigidly.…The screaming and moaning of the girls could be heard for a square."

For some time, the girls' families feared that they might die. Dr. Woody insisted they were just "nervous," had suffered from nothing more serious than a good grossing-out and that they would recover. Since their names do not appear in subsequent obituaries with sarcastic headlines—as, again, was custom at the time—it seems his diagnosis was correct.

TATERS AND GRAVEY

Why waste good farmland? That was the attitude of unsqueamish farmers who lived near Shelbyville, Shelby County. According to a November 1873 report in the local paper, every spring they would uproot tombstones and plant potatoes on the land fertilized by the bodies of their former fellow citizens. After the crops were taken up months later, the farmers would replace the tombstones—in the correct places, one hopes.

SAINTS PRESERVE US

In the autumn of 1873, coffins unearthed in the Whitehead graveyard in Claysville, Harrison County, were taken to Cynthiana's Battle Grove Cemetery for reburial. On November 10, diggers found the metal casket of Dr. William Curran's two-year-old daughter Mary, who died on July 1, 1855. Someone opened it and onlookers were astounded to see that the child was in perfect condition except for a sunken eye, a missing nose and a shrunken upper lip. Most amazingly, two damask rosebuds that had been placed on the child's chest at burial had blossomed somehow into "beautiful full-blown roses" with green leaves. One of the witnesses was the child's father, who carried the coffin home. Being dead yet perfectly preserved was one way to get famous in 1873, and Dr. Curran's office was soon the locus of curiosity seekers. On November 15, he took the body to a Mrs. M. Shumate's house in Cynthiana prior to its reburial. Hundreds turned out to drink in this wonder.

Another case occurred in the same general location. Mrs. Richard Cummins passed away in the autumn of 1860 and was placed in a metallic casket—the ineffably unnerving-looking old-fashioned kind with a face window—and placed in the Lair family vault on the bank of the South Licking River in Harrison County. In the spring of 1861, she was removed and placed in the graveyard on North Main Street in Cynthiana. There she passed the time until May 21, 1907, when she was exhumed for reburial in Battle Grove Cemetery. Her excavators peeped into that foggy pane of glass and marveled to see that Mrs. Cummins was lifelike, right down "a slight bloom appearing on the cheek."

A MAN BURIED IN Paducah, McCracken County, in 1856 was exhumed in August 1880. He looked almost the same as he had on the day he had been planted, except now he had a most becoming eighteen-inch beard.

MARGARET BRISBY WAS INTERRED in the Lutheran burying ground in Fayette County in 1856. She was exhumed for reburial in Lexington Cemetery, appropriately on the day before Halloween, 1907. When the metallic coffin's lid creaked open, impressed witnesses saw that "the features of the dead woman were still recognizable and that the white lace cap on the head of the corpse was perfectly preserved and as neat and fresh in appearance as it was when placed in the coffin more than fifty years ago." Her face appeared as solid and fixed as marble.

MURRAY WALKER WAS EXHUMED at Valley Hill, Washington County, on August 6, 1908, to be reburied next to his recently deceased wife in Pleasant Grove Cemetery. Though Walker died in 1866, he was in such good shape that it was thought his clothes could still be worn.

FOUR MEMBERS OF THE McDonald-Glass family were to be removed from the abandoned graveyard at Sixteenth and Jefferson Streets in Louisville in November 1915 and reburied in Cave Hill Cemetery. One of them, Daniel McDonald, dead since 1868, had a surprise for his descendants.

When his grave was opened on November 15, he was in perfect condition, with the addition of a foot-long beard he didn't have when buried. Witnesses had to look fast, though. Almost as soon as he was exposed to air, Mr. McDonald crumbled to dust.

MRS. YOUNG DIED OF cholera in Paris, Bourbon County, in summer 1854. In April 1872, her family wanted her reburied in Mount Sterling, Montgomery County, where they had moved. No one was certain if the correct grave had been unearthed, but Mrs. Young's grown daughters said they could identify her by her crescent-shaped earrings. The coffin was brought to the surface—the iron plate covering the glass window was removed—and the daughters were gratified to see not the expected skeleton but a woman in an ideal state except for sunken eyes and a slight yellowish hue that even tinted the wreath on her chest. She still had rosebuds in her hair.

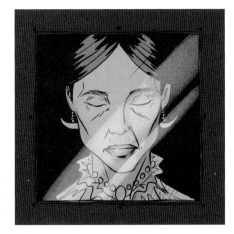

ON APRIL 24, 1969, workers digging a septic tank line on the site of the Egypt Plantation in Cruger, Mississippi, unearthed a long-forgotten and unmarked grave four feet below the surface. The body-shaped Fisk metal casket had a glass window plate, and through it astonished workers saw the perfectly preserved face of a beautiful woman in her twenties with long black or brown hair. When the coffin was opened, they found she was dressed in an expensive red velvet dress, complete with a cape and buckled shoes, according to columnist Brian Broom. She also wore white gloves. The secret of her remarkable preservation: the casket had been filled with alcohol before burial. No one in 1969 had the slightest idea of the woman's identity, nor does anyone know now. She was reburied in the Odd Fellows Cemetery in Lexington, Mississippi, under a marker memorializing her as the "Lady in Red."

The Fisk casket—one of the creepiest coffin designs *ever*—was patented in 1848 and went on sale in 1849. Shoe experts have observed that the style the

Lady in Red wore was common before the Civil War, so whoever she was, she must have died between roughly 1849 and 1860. For what it's worth, I can provide details of a similar case from the same era and region involving a Kentucky native.

Mary Jane Helm was born in Hardin County in 1810, the sister of Governor John LaRue Helm. In 1833, she married Patrick Tompkins in Hardin County; later, he became a congressman in Mississippi. She died in Vicksburg on February 14, 1840. Though the Fisk casket had not been invented yet, she was interred with great care in a zinc coffin full of alcohol, which was placed in a larger outer wooden coffin. The whole thing was further packed in charcoal. She was exhumed on February 27, 1857, to be reburied in Cedar Hill Cemetery in Vicksburg. Like the Lady in Red, she was in splendid condition, "features natural, and hair as flexible as in life."

AT REST—NOT

Edward Fible of Louisville, age nineteen and in excellent health, woke up on the morning of October 6, 1895, feeling just swell. Later in the morning, he suddenly got sick and went back to bed. His sister, Hattie Bowman, sent for help. Edward died soon after Dr. Taylor's arrival.

A few hours after Edward's abrupt illness and demise, a woman noticed that his leg seemed to be moving. She raised the sheet. His leg gave "a sudden jerk." Until late in the afternoon, Fible's corpse was in motion: "The arms and legs were thrown about as if the man were in agony, and the toes and fingers worked rapidly." At one point, he nearly turned over on his side.

The puzzled Dr. Taylor detected neither respiration nor heartbeat. He called in his colleague Dr. Galvin to see the show, but neither could explain the corpse's calisthenics. The obvious explanation is the onset of rigor mortis, but this condition begins at the head and not the lower extremities. A woman who attended Edward's deathbed, and who was a frequent Fible houseguest, had had three insured husbands die in a strange manner. Rumor held that she poisoned Edward for profit. That would explain the sudden death of a healthy young man, but while he was insured, it was for only $137, and the beneficiary was his sister Hattie, not the woman in question.

There were no further news stories, so we can conclude that the coroner found neither poison nor an explanation for Fible's flailing.

DOING THE TWIST

One day in April 1874, the gardener of the cemetery at Georgetown did a double take, perhaps a triple take. Near the graveyard's center was the enormous marble monument of one of Scott County's wealthiest former residents (unnamed in the original article, more's the pity), and when the gardener gazed upon it, he saw that the engraved name and age of the deceased were not where they should have been. It was as though they had been obliterated. The amazed landscaper looked several times, even touching the monument to feel for the missing letters. He got another surprise when he walked around the marble stone and found the inscription on the *opposite* side. The only explanation that seemed feasible was that many people—for one person could not have done it—joined forces and twisted the monument around to face the reverse direction. But there were no signs that such labor had been undertaken, nor could anyone explain *why* it should be done.

TURNING THE CORONER

Len Faxon, newspaperman, decided in 1874 to run for office as Paducah's coroner. He thus described his qualifications: "An experience of several years within the precincts of Cairo [Illinois] render me an excellent judge of a dead man."

BODY SHAMING

In the sultry month of June 1874, Louisville residents who lived at the foot of Clay Street, near the Ohio River, noticed the repellant fragrance of rotting garbage. An inspection unearthed human skeletal remains, including two adult male skulls. Someone with a sparkling sense of humor stuck a hat on one and placed it atop a pole to the delightful staccato shrieks of passing girls. Were the dead men murder victims or missing persons? How had their remains gotten mixed up with the compost? City sanitation officials neither knew nor cared to find out. The skeletons were collected along with the trash, and all was sunk in the river. "This, to say the least of it, is a somewhat inglorious ending of a life's career," remarked the *Courier-Journal*.

PANIC POEM

In the summer of 1858, an experimental gentleman vowed to spend a few days in Mammoth Cave. His nerves couldn't handle the strain even one day. The next morning, when the guide carried in the man's breakfast, he found the experimenter "in a state of high excitement and great terror" and he fled without taking his meal. But he did try to capture his feelings for posterity in a lengthy and dreary poem, his way of admitting that Mammoth Cave was too much for him. He even implied that the wrath of God would be preferable to spending a night there. The poem began and ended as follows:

> *Again 'tis morn, I know,*
> *For long and weary vigils had I kept,*
> *Ere sleep did bless my eyes.*
> *I thought of night, and of Boeotian darkness....*
> *Oh! could I feel a gentle breath from Bethlehem's babe*
> *Or even feel a Sinai tremble with an angry God!*

I'M NOT A MOURNING PERSON

Twenty-six-year-old Robert Frank Merrick of Caldwell County impersonated a detective and forged checks in Illinois. He was arrested on November 19, 1900, and confessed. His wife, the former Cora Reese, whom he had married the previous January 3 when she was all of thirteen years old, immediately filed for divorce. To top Frank's litany of woe, he was so ill that he was confined at home in Caldwell County rather than taken to jail. It might seem as though his life could go no further downhill, but things can always get worse. He died "in agony" surrounded by lawmen on November 24.

But the night after his burial, someone broke into Frank's grave in Blue Spring Church Cemetery at Hopson for reasons unknown. Perhaps his body was stolen. Also, on the same day his less-than-mournful widow married James Moore. It was an eventful day for all concerned.

Frank's cousin James Merrick lived near the graveyard and insisted that he made secret marks on the mound to ascertain whether anyone attempted grave robbery since he expected that someone might try it. The next morning, James found unmistakable signs that an intruder had performed an unauthorized exhumation. Neighbors said they saw a covered wagon leaving the cemetery in the dead of night, heading in the direction of Cadiz, the driver not sparing the whip. "At any rate, the grave has undoubtedly been tampered with," said a reporter.

The rumor mill ground out juicy speculation. Some thought Frank Merrick had killed himself after the disgrace of arrest; others, that he faked his death; or perhaps, he died but was not buried. Most interestingly, many wondered about the sudden onset of Frank's illness and death and suspected that he had been poisoned. Authorities called for an official inquiry, which would require exhuming Frank and removing his entrails to check for traces of poison. Had a murderer body-snatched Merrick to prevent his bowels from being examined? Adding to the speculation, while Merrick had been out in Illinois forging checks, his estranged wife swore openly that she had fallen in love with James Moore and would marry him. To some observers, this seemed suspicious.

The matter was never settled satisfactorily since Frank's father insisted the body was still in the grave and refused to allow an investigation, making "dire threats" against anyone who tried. The final guess was that the coffin had been exhumed but reburied with the body still inside. This theory maintained that Frank's widow, Cora, with or without an accomplice, opened the grave to make sure he was dead since she was about to get remarried. After all, if it turned out her first husband was alive somewhere, that could lead to social embarrassment. Better to be a ghoul than a bigamist because people might talk! Mr. Moore said his new bride insisted that medical students had nabbed Frank.

Who knows? On Resurrection Day, Frank might pop up in some completely unexpected location.

A MODEL CITIZEN MODELS

John C. Latham, born in Hopkinsville in 1844, became a wealthy banker and philanthropist. He died in New York City on August 18, 1909, and was sent home for burial. After the fact, citizens wanted a statue made of their esteemed native son and benefactor, but that would entail disturbing his eternal slumber. The widow gave permission, and in September a sculptor entered the mausoleum with the materials necessary for making a plaster cast of Mr. Latham's face.

BUSY

Falmouth, Pendleton County, must not have been too large a city 150 years ago, since Charles F. Broseke served as the town's hotelkeeper, undertaker, justice of the peace and coroner. On one memorable day, September 11, 1875, he plied all four trades. Nicholas Lovelace shot and killed Moses Lockhart in Broseke's Bodman House hotel. As justice of the peace, Broseke summoned a jury; as coroner, he held an inquest and scrutinized the corpse of his murdered guest; as undertaker, he buried Lockhart.

THE DEAD'S THREADS

Circa August 1876, an elderly man in Greenup County entered the sleep that knows no dreaming. The *Greenup Independent* reported with righteous indignation that after the mourners left, the man's son slinked back to the cemetery, opened the grave and stole the suit his father was buried in, thinking it too nice to go to waste. The editor said that the thrifty ghoul not

only wore the suit in public but also openly boasted about how he obtained it. The family of recently deceased William Riley must have thought the article was referring to one of them, because they had him exhumed to prove that he still wore his final finery. The newspaper quickly clarified in *italics*, perhaps out of healthy fear of a libel lawsuit, "[A] report lately brought through our columns regarding the robbing of a grave *had no reference to Mr. William Riley or his family*."

A similar incident had occurred elsewhere some twenty-five years earlier. A man died on a steamboat in the summer of 1851 and was buried in Paducah Cemetery. In April 1852, the man's son traveled from Missouri and had him exhumed to see if any valuables had accompanied him to the grave. The corpse's money belt was empty, but he had $700 in his pocket—in modern currency, that would be equivalent to $17,600, thus the son's understandable insistence on disturbing his father's rest.

STUDENT BODIES

Students named U.A. Thompson and Burrell Heidelberg died at Georgetown University in the summer of 1854 and were buried in an old local cemetery. They were exhumed on June 9, 1910, and reburied in Georgetown Cemetery. The weird part is that they weren't relocated by professional undertakers but by members of their fraternity, Tau Theta Kappa.

BIZARRE BURIALS

Workmen unearthing the grave of Judge Paul Jones Booker's stepmother in Springfield, Washington County, in December 1874 got a surprise: the skeleton of an unknown person who had been unceremoniously dumped in the grave and then covered with dirt. Mrs. Booker's coffin was intact. No one ever figured out the skeleton's identity, but likely it was a murder victim stashed in a perfect hiding place, for who would open a grave to look for the body of someone who wasn't supposed to be there? It was noted that a year and a half after Mrs. Booker died in December 1826, an ornamental rock tomb was placed on her grave. So whoever the mystery man was, he must have been stashed there during that time.

EIGHTEEN-YEAR-OLD RUTH HARPER OF Carlisle, Nicholas County, was killed in a car wreck on May 5, 1927, while on her way home from purchasing a high school graduation robe. She was buried in it.

SEVENTY-TWO-YEAR-OLD INEZ BRADMORE OF Baltimore fell fatally ill on a train journey to Boyd County. She said that she desired to be buried among the lovely hills of eastern Kentucky. After she died at King's Daughter's Hospital, she was given a full ceremony in Ashland Cemetery on March 19, 1929, "in spite of the fact that fate brought her to Ashland to die with only a few dollars in her purse."

JAMES T. COOK OF 944 South Preston Street, Louisville, got an unwelcome surprise after a gas meter reader observed a depression in the earth of his cellar on August 13, 1925. Patrolman Benjamin Smith and Mr. Cook commenced digging on August 14—being careful not to strike an estimated twenty-five busybodies who crowded into the basement to watch—and two feet down, they unearthed a fancy comb and a woman's shoe. At a depth of seven feet, they found part of a decayed human rib, a fragment of a spine, clumps of brown hair and the dilapidated remains of a broken pine coffin. Judging from the smallness of the bones and the three-foot casket length, the unmarked grave was a child's final resting place. A former cemetery

sexton who inspected the relics noted that the coffin wood was unfinished and the nails homemade, so whoever built the casket, dug the grave and buried the child was a do-it-yourselfer. The remains were never identified. The coroner suggested that a medical student had thus disposed of a body after dissecting it, but I think it was the handiwork of some past miser who didn't want to alert the authorities or undergo the expense of a cemetery plot.

HOMEOPATHIC DOCTOR AND LEXINGTON citizen J.H.A. Fehr died of cholera in Louisville in the summer of 1851. He was an atheist, so no hymns for Fehr! He stipulated in his will that a band play "Home, Sweet Home" as his remains were lowered into the awaiting earth.

SOMETIME IN THE AUTUMN of 1852, a German boy died in Jefferson County. His stepfather purchased a boot container for his remains rather than a casket, figuring that was good enough. Then he found that the box was too short by a good six inches. The stepfather could have procured a longer box, of course, but a quick trip to the toolbox provided a simpler alternative, much to the exasperation of the child's mother.

DESPITE FAILING HEALTH IN the spring of 1899, invalid William Saulsberry of Aden, Carter County, was determined to have a final resting place worth talking about. Specifically, he ordered construction of a watertight vault with eight-inch-thick walls and "an asphalt slab [which] will be cemented over the coffin, resting on a four-inch projection inside the wall, which will also be covered with cement to make an airtight receptacle for the casket." It

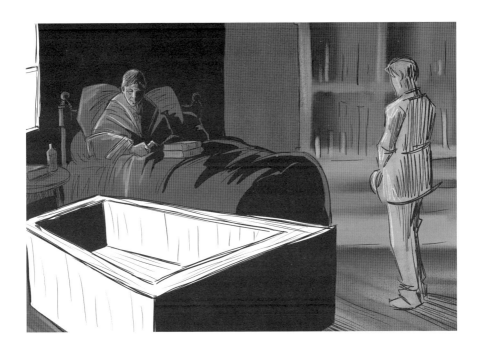

would have an arched roof to allow rain to run off. The whole thing was to be level with a hillside's surface. On April 25, workmen carried the majestic casket Saulsberry purchased into his bedroom so he could caress it with his eyes. He died on April 29 at age sixty-one, having been unable to check out personally construction of his tomb in progress.

Similarly, Colonel Jim Browder of Fulton County had his tomb carved into solid rock in 1904. He lay down in it to make sure it would fit his coffin. Then he further tested the crypt by keeping a piece of meat in it for a year. He was satisfied, and there he was entombed when he died on September 10, 1906—wrapped in forty yards of linen, which he also had purchased in advance.

WILLIAM STEELE OF ABERDEEN, Butler County, fell off a flatboat and drowned on December 4, 1856. All efforts to find the body failed, but on the night of February 5, 1857, his neighbor James Potts dreamed that he caught the body. He had the same dream the following night. On February 7, Potts took a walk to contemplate a riverside garden once cultivated by the late Mr. Steele and to retrieve a skiff tethered there that was at risk of being carried away by ice. When Potts cleared away the ice, he found the body of Steele floating in an eddy. Potts pulled the corpse from the water, just as he had dreamed, and Steele's postmortem homecoming culminated in his getting a Christian burial on February 8.

THE BURIAL CEREMONY OF a young Irish girl named Burke in Louisville on July 16, 1858, furnished an unsightly spectacle. She was to be placed in the same grave in which her brother had been interred several years before, so there was the hole with the casket barely covered at the bottom. The girl's mother said she wanted to see her dearly departed son again, so another son—who was drunk—leaped into the grave with a handy pick and broke open the lid. He held up a bone and slurred "Do you see that?" Everyone *did* see that and persuaded him to climb out of the hole. But he jumped in again after his sister's coffin was lowered. A third brother was heard to remark that he would like to shoot the inebriated so-and-so. Mr. Burke was subsequently charged with public intoxication, not to mention spectacular disorderly conduct, and sentenced to the workhouse.

A. IRWIN LAMPTON SHOT himself in the heart in Louisville's United States Hotel on June 23, 1858. The man, who was handicapped, left eloquent suicide notes and a final request: he wanted to go to his grave unwashed, and he desired a doctor to cut his sinews so his legs could be straightened out at last.

HAIRBREADTH ESCAPES

On the evening of Saturday, August 12, 1854, Father Maguire of the Catholic Church in Lexington noticed that pieces of plaster had fallen off the ceiling. After the congregation gathered next morning, he decided to cancel the rest of the service. After all, falling flakes of plaster might spook people, and in any case, it could ruin their fine clothing. Not long after the last person exited, the entire ceiling collapsed, raining heavy crossbeams where the worshipers had been sitting.

LOUISVILLE WAS PLAGUED BY a rash of burglaries in the summer of 1859. In one thrilling incident, a young man who lived on Seventh Street stepped out of his house on the night of June 2 and was slashed by a marauder. The knife was deflected by a stack of love letters in the man's pocket. The would-be victim happened to be carrying an antiquated horse pistol loaded with small shot with which he intended to shoot rats, and instead, he used it to warm the hide of his fleeing attacker.

ON MARCH 3, 1855, the *Louisville Courier* mentioned a rumor that two graduating medical students were spoiling to fight a duel that very day. One of them hinted that he also wanted to fight a faculty member who upbraided him for smoking a cigar. Certainly it would have been an interesting duel, since the newly minted doctors' hard-earned medical knowledge indicated just where to aim weapons to do the most damage. But the young cadaver carvers changed their minds, as the *Courier* noted with wry disappointment on March 5: "We beg the pardon of our readers for not furnishing them a particularly bloody item this morning."

An inconsequential duel occurred in Hardin County in December 1856. Perhaps I am misreading the news account, but it sounds as though one

participant soiled his breeches from fear: "A shooting affray occurred at Troutman's Ferry, on the Rolling Fork, a few days since; but the particulars as narrated to us, partake quite as much of the ludicrous as of the tragic. No damage done, except to the clothes of one of the parties."

BONES OF CONTENTION

Jonathan Simpson Jr., age twenty-three, died of cholera in Louisville on August 15, 1851. His body was brought home to Bardstown, Nelson County, in an airtight zinc coffin to keep the contagion in check. On August 20, the *Louisville Courier* published a letter from an angry anonymous writer calling himself (or herself, who knows?) "Bardstown," who claimed that the city's trustees refused Simpson burial since he had died of a highly communicable disease, regardless of his fancy zinc coffin; in fact, they had ordered his body not be brought into town at all. "Bardstown" ridiculed the trustees as "sapient grannies" and deemed their actions "worthy of the palmiest days of witchcraft and blue laws." The author was quick to add that the town fathers' panicky decision was unpopular among citizens. The *Courier*'s editors called the refusal to bury Simpson "barbarism" and remarked, "The action of the trustees…is a piece of heartless cruelty not often equaled. It is without excuse or palliation."

Three days later, the *Courier* published a blistering editorial from the *Madison Banner* as well as a note written by Simpson's heartbroken father, which seemed to corroborate the charge. Simpson Sr. claimed that he and some friends had to bury the body in the suburbs themselves, in the dark of night. In the same issue, the *Courier* published a letter signed by the much-abused trustees—one of whom was amusingly named J.M. Doom— indignantly protesting that "Bardstown's" letter was "false throughout." Their version of events held that on the contrary, they wanted the body to be buried immediately upon arrival, and citizens *did too* object to having a man who had died of cholera in their midst. They ended their letter on a note of eloquent annoyance: "[A]ll journals of the day should be more cautious how they publish and endorse writings they know nothing about." It's the kind of thing that makes you not want to run for public office.

Then came another letter from Simpson's father, published on August 25, elegantly hinting that the trustees were a bunch of liars. That appears to have been the final word on the controversy. One thing is certain: Jonathan Simpson Jr. definitely is buried in Bardstown's Old Presbyterian Cemetery *now*. Whether he always was, is another matter.

BUSTED!

Black Union soldiers were a novelty in September 1865, so it was news when they occupied the Oldham County Courthouse yard. They left on September 18, and when officials inspected the building the next day, another novelty ensued: they reportedly found the corpse of an unidentified White woman in a coffin, "placed there very recently." A few days later came the sheepish admission that the "corpse" was a statue bust of a man and the "murder" was a foolish rumor that made its way into print.

GUESSING IN RHYME

When Mary Ann Cecil died in Spencer County, the stonecutter had no idea what age to carve on her tombstone. So he had to estimate:

She bid adieu to all that was alive
In the year of 1845;
And how old she was we had that to fix,
She was near the age of 76.

KEGGER

The spring 1869 *Louisville Courier-Journal* story was horrifying. A Chicago malt salesman named L.A. Gerbier had come to the city on January 5 to conduct business with the city's numerous brewers. A few days later, he vanished. All anyone knew was that Gerbier had last been seen in a city brewery. The mystery was solved on March 30, when a man choked on a swallow of beer in a Green Street saloon. A doctor was called and extracted

a human toe from the drinker's throat. Detectives wondered if the missing L.A. Gerbier had been murdered and his body disposed of in the brewery. They confiscated the saloon's offending keg and, upon opening it, found a pinky finger.

No doubt many Louisvillian beer drinkers initially had second thoughts about imbibing the local product, especially that served on Green Street. But if they contemplated the date of the story's appearance—April Fool's Day—they may have become doubtful. And if they looked closely at the name of the alleged missing man, L.A. Gerbier, perhaps they saw that it was uncomfortably close to *lager beer*.

The next day, the paper assured readers that Mr. Gerbier had last been seen in the company of H.I. Ghwines and L. Ondonporter, and three lowlifes named Weiskie, Damschnapps and Al K. Hall were under suspicion. For the benefit of readers who still hadn't grasped the joke, it added: "The detectives are confident that the case will be fully worked up by the first of April next."

Until the joke was revealed, alcohol sales in the city fell by 90 percent, or so it was said.

A TWICE-TOLD TALE

The story that circulated in December 1865 was that Mrs. Heady had sold land in Union County and made a couple thousand dollars. A couple of days later, a traveling stranger stopped and asked if he could lodge there for the night. Mrs. Heady was reluctant but finally agreed. Good thing, too, because in the wee hours she heard someone trying to break in. The stranger took his pistol and told her to open the front door, but to stand behind it. He shot three disguised men in rapid succession as they entered, killing two and wounding one. One dead burglar was Mrs. Heady's son-in-law and the other a neighbor.

A ripping yarn! But in July 1870 the *Louisville Commercial* reported that at Mount Washington, Bullitt County, a wayfarer staying overnight at a newly wealthy widow's house shot three or more would-be burglars, one of whom turned out to be her brother-in-law. Conclusion: either similar incidents happened twice or the whole thing was an urban legend to begin with. In fact, a contemporary dismissed the Bullitt County version as "an old story, taken from *Hoofland's Almanac*."

CATGUT STRINGS? NO, MANGUT

A man who died in Columbus, Hickman County, in the autumn of 1872 requested in his will that his money go to establishing a "cat infirmary." He also asked that his intestines be made into fiddle strings and that said instrument be played for the feline inmates' entertainment "forever and ever, without cessation day or night." Some suspected he might have been insane.

WHEN SARCASM IS UNCALLED FOR

African American residents of Harrodsburg were in a lather of fear in late January 1872. They had heard rumors that a Black body snatcher named Bill Simms (or Sim) was looking for corpses to sell to medical schools. Allegedly, he received $250 for healthy specimens of the dead, $100 for sickly ones and $300 for *live* persons for doctors' vivisection experiments. Since snatchers plundered so many Black graves during the era, one can understand the citizenry's anxiety and willingness to believe the worst of Simms.

The gossip started when Simms merely helped move the body of a Black pauper from his grave to a doctor's dissection room. Mobs threatened Simms, who sneered at them and did not help his case by saying that *yes*, he was there to kidnap the living and the dead, and he had done it many times before, and he wouldn't stop until he had collected six more anatomical subjects and had cleared $1,000. The contemptuous humor was lost on his audience. A man named Sol Bunton added fuel to the fire by claiming that Simms had tried to abduct him, but Simms countered that he was just trying to have fun by scaring Bunton.

On the night of February 2, T.W. Foster, who lived just north of town, heard a volley of gunshots. Stepping outside, he saw a crowd of angry Black men who said they were hunting for Simms. They insisted on searching Foster's cellar and, not finding their prey, left the premises. But the next day, Foster found blood in the forest near his house, firing speculation that the mob found the rumored resurrectionist and lynched him, which could mean anything ranging from a whipping to outright murder. Simms was never seen again, at least in that vicinity, so he may have paid for his sarcasm with his life.

BOONE'S BONES, OR HAVE A LITTLE BACKBONE

In 1870, a newspaper correspondent recalled when the remains of pioneer Daniel Boone and his wife, having been exhumed in Missouri, were reburied with great fanfare in Frankfort Cemetery in July 1845. He told readers a long-kept secret: he had been present when Boone was briefly dug up again in 1860 so a monument could be added to the grave. The gravedigger tossed up portions of rotten coffin wood, ribs, tibias, fibulas, vertebrae, even a hipbone. When no one was looking, the writer snatched one of the explorer's lumbar vertebrae and kept it. At least his conscience troubled him: "But that bit of moldy backbone laid heavily on my conscience. I couldn't look an honest man in the face as long as I had it." He finally buried it to assuage his guilty feelings.

There has been a controversy for decades that Missouri may have sent the wrong remains to Kentucky; thus, the body in Daniel Boone's grave may not be his after all. If not, the joke was on the souvenir-seeking journalist.

A Different Kind of Pioneer Story

Indian attacks were not uncommon in Kentucky's earliest days. In Hardin County, pioneers gathered for safety in Linder's Fort on Hardin Creek. Possibly because of the cramped quarters and relentless anxiety, two settlers, Isaac Hynes and John Parker, came to a mutual detestation. They called each other "traitor" and each often threatened to murder the other. Their fellow pioneers took the promises of violence so seriously that they hid the fort's supply of bullets and lead. However, the resourceful Hynes melted a pewter spoon, molded it into a bullet, and shot Parker in the heart one morning while everyone was at breakfast. The fort's inhabitants arrested and tried and acquitted Hynes since Parker had threatened him so often.

Parker was buried in the fort's cemetery, and his inconsolable dog sat by the grave night and day, even excavating the mound to a depth of two feet in doggish hopes that he might again see his master.

BIBLIOGRAPHY

1. Snatched: Louisville Resurrectionists

Kaltenbacher, Will S. "Ghouls Grow Obsolete." *Louisville Courier-Journal*, December 31, 1922.

Louisville Courier. "The Body Snatching Case." February 5, 1857.

———. "A Mysterious Disappearance." January 28, 1857, 3.

———. "Police Court." February 7, 1857.

Louisville Courier-Journal. "Body Identified." September 12, 1871.

———. "'Body Snatching' and 'Grave Robbing.'" August 7, 1871.

———. "A Corpseless Coffin." August 6, 1871.

———. "The Corpse Not There." January 7, 1885.

———. "A Corpse Swims." November 30, 1868.

———. "The Corpse That the Brother Came After…" September 7, 1871.

———. "Corpses Are Rented." March 3, 1896.

———. "The Dissecting Room." November 30, 1868.

———. "Dissecting-Room Agent." February 21, 1894.

———. "The Dissecting Room Mystery." April 8, 1870.

———. "Flynn's Body Found." June 12, 1891.

———. "From Frankfort." April 19, 1873.

———. "The Goldsticker Case." January 9, 1885.

———. "Grewsome." March 2, 1896.

———. "His Hair Turned Gray." October 5, 1884.

———. "In a Pickling Vat." June 11, 1891.

———. "Is It Goldsticker's Body?" January 8, 1885.

———. "Jennie Robinson's Will." June 11, 1902.

———. "Medical Horrors." April 18, 1875.

———. "A Medical Sensation." December 7, 1872.

———. "No Bond." December 2, 1902.

———. "Not Good for a Steady Diet." June 6, 1874.

———. "Short Stock." December 3, 1902.

———. "Singular Incident." March 26, 1870.

———. "'Snatching.'" December 1, 1902.

———. "A Spectral Scene." August 23, 1881.

———. "Stolen from the Dead Room." December 11, 1885.

———. "Subjects." May 16, 1870.

———. "An Uninviting Plate of Sausage." January 18, 1876.

———. "Very Sad, and True." July 19, 1874.

———. "A Victim of Science." September 10, 1871.

2. Plight of the Living Dead: Premature Burial

Louisville Courier. "Another Terrible Warning." August 16, 1849.

Louisville Courier-Journal. "Asleep or Dead?" December 4, 1876.

———. "A Cholera Incident of 1833." July 19, 1873.

———. "The Corpse Came To." August 9, 1887.

———. "Dead Woman Speaks to Crowd at Wake." February 9, 1907.

———. "Didn't Want to Be Buried." April 25, 1876.

———. "*Georgetown Times*." March 10, 1876.

———. "Girl Returns to Life." March 12, 1904.

———. "In His Coffin for the Second Time." March 27, 1888.

———. "Is It a Corpse?" December 3, 1876.

———. "Laura Rothfield Was Buried." December 7, 1876.

———. "Not Much of a Dead Man." April 18, 1869.

———."A Peculiar Case." January 27, 1885.

———. "Richmond." January 25, 1882.

———. "She Was Not Dead, But Only in a Trance." October 14, 1903.

———. "The Singular Sleeper." December 5, 1876.

———. "Strange, If True." June 23, 1886.

———. "Supposed Corpse Sits Up." November 19, 1912.

———. "Suspended Animation." February 17, 1894.

———. "There Was No Change…" December 6, 1874.

———. "Undertaker Withdraws When 'Corpse' Breathes." September 18, 1916.

3. The Tragedy of Lester

Louisville Courier-Journal. "Bringing Lester Bryant's Body Home…" January 22, 1913.
———. "Bryant Monument Suggested." January 28, 1913.
——— . "Bryant's Body at Home." January 23, 1913.
———. "Champion Corn Grower of Kentucky and His Teacher." January 14, 1913.
———. "Department Blameless." January 24, 1913.
———. "Fifty-Three Ears Sold…" February 13, 1913.
———. "Kentucky Corn Champion Dead." January 21, 1913.
———. "Lester Bryant." Editorial. January 22, 1913.
———. "Lester Bryant." Editorial. January 24, 1913.
———. "Lester Bryant Is Eulogized." February 12, 1913.
———. "Lester Bryant's Funeral Largely Attended." January 24, 1913.
———. "Lester Bryant's Untimely End." January 25, 1913.
———. "Memorial to Champion." February 12, 1913.
———. "Official Statement of Facts…" January 26, 1913.
———. "Poor Prospects for Bryant Monument." February 1, 1913.
———. "Stone in Memory of Lamented Lester Bryant." August 16, 1914.

4. Peculiarly Perishing

Augusta (GA) Chronicle. "A Lamentable Occurrence." April 4, 1835.
Louisville Courier. "Accidentally Killed." May 2, 1861.
———. "Another Scrape." July 22, 1858.
———. "Attempt at Suicide." April 9, 1856.
———. "By Referring to Our Police Report…" November 30, 1852.
———. "Carl Loveday…" May 15, 1858.
———. "Dr. J.C. Gunn." April 22, 1858.
———. "A Dramatic Death." December 2, 1848.
———. "Effects of Jealousy." July 10, 1854.
———. "Fatal Accident." September 6, 1855.
———. "Fatal Mistake." June 16, 1856.
———. "In New Orleans…" April 18, 1855.
———. "Inquest." November 29, 1852.
———. "Jefferson Circuit Court." December 14, 1852.
———. "Killed." May 28, 1853.

———. "The Largest Funeral Procession…" November 29, 1852.

———. "Loveday Discharged." April 23, 1858.

———. "A Man Named Lough…" January 15, 1855.

———. "The Maysville…" August 14, 1860.

———. "Melancholy." February 3, 1853.

———. "One or Two Points That May Be Considered…" December 17, 1852.

———. "An Outrage." July 30, 1857.

———. "Poisoning." April 29, 1854.

———. "Police Court." November 30, 1852.

———. "A Printer at Cincinnati…" October 15, 1859.

———. "Remarkable Suicide." April 23, 1858.

———. "Sad Occurrence." July 9, 1859.

———. "Sudden Death." November 29, 1852.

Louisville Courier-Journal. "Another Porkishly-Inclined…" April 22, 1869.

———. "Bowling Green Youth Is Killed by Javelin." April 23, 1935.

———. "Boy, 14, Shot at Game Sinking." September 25, 1927.

———. "Boy Shot Watching Football Game." September 24, 1927.

———. "Criminal Folly." August 6, 1873.

———. "Death on the Bridge." August 15, 1875.

———. "Dies After Eating Buzzard." October 23, 1907.

———. "An Extraordinary Death." November 17, 1873.

———. "George Shout…" April 1, 1873.

———. "In Maysville." July 22, 1873.

———. "James W. Godman…" February 8, 1875.

———. "Lexington." April 9, 1869.

———. "Lexington *Gazette*." August 2, 1875.

———. "The *Lexington Gazette* Says…" April 11, 1869.

———. "The *Lexington Observer and Reporter* Says…" April 20, 1869.

———. "The *Lexington Statesman* Says…" April 10, 1869.

———. "A Negro Inventor's End." September 9, 1874.

———. "People Should Be Careful…" October 3, 1876.

———. "Prisoner Buried by Tons of Rock." May 11, 1921.

———. "Railroad Brakeman Decapitated." August 31, 1918.

———. "Said Good-Bye." July 27, 1902.

———. "Stephen [*sic*] A. Jones…" February 20, 1871.

———. "Strangled." March 25, 1900.

———. "Teacher Fined $500 in Student's Death." February 17, 1928.

———. "There Is a Report Floating About…" April 17, 1869.

———. "Will Laugh Herself to Death." November 16, 1893.

———. "Workman at Camp Knox…" November 13, 1918.
———. "Youth's Curiosity May Result in His Death." November 22, 1916.
Louisville Journal. "Deaths by Lightning." July 23, 1842.
———. "Killed by a Paper Wad." February 22, 1868.
———. "Killed by Lightning." July 27, 1866.
———. "Lightning and the Beech Tree." February 3, 1843.
———. "A Man…" February 2, 1843.
———. "A Man by the Name of Nolin…" February 1, 1864.
———. "A New Game to Play." January 13, 1849.
———. "A Sad Accident…" April 10, 1865.
———. "Upwards of Two Weeks Ago…" May 16, 1865.
Owensboro Messenger and Examiner. "The Gun Was Loaded." November 1, 1888.

5. My Old Kentucky (Haunted) Home

Harris, Lee B. *Kentucky Real Estate Professionals and the Law*. N.p.: Thomson-West, 2004.
Lebanon Standard. "A Strange Suicide." December 25, 1872, n.p.
Louisville Courier. "Haunted House in Newport…" July 4, 1855.
———. "Murder of a Person Supposed to be From Cincinnati." January 24, 1853.
Louisville Courier-Journal. "Attempted Assassination." August 13, 1870.
———. "Brutal Murder in Daviess [*sic*] County." January 8, 1874.
———. "Fee at a Funeral." January 21, 1895.
———. "From the Other World." February 5, 1874.
———. "A Genuine Haunted House in Hickman County." February 5, 1873.
———. "Ghosts in Greenup." June 23, 1895.
———. "Ghosts in the House." January 29, 1895.
———. "Ghosts Keep Many Houses from Getting Tenants." March 13, 1905.
———. "The Grand Jury Yesterday…" September 6, 1870.
———. "Harrodsburg People." September 5, 1874.
———. "A Haunted House." November 27, 1891.
———. "In the Police Court Yesterday…" August 16, 1870.
———. "The Jail Spook." October 3, 1895.
———. "A Kentucky Ghost." July 9, 1874.
———. "The Late Tragedy." August 15, 1870.
———. "A Marion County Sensation." March 8, 1873.
———. "Mike Callahan…" September 22, 1870.

———. "Mob Law in Muhlenberg." January 14, 1874.

———. "Negroes Terrified by House Believed to Be Haunted." September 12, 1904.

———. "The Peddler's Grave." March 19, 1883.

———. "Saw Dilger's Ghost." November 13, 1898.

———. "Spook With the Corpse." January 20, 1895.

———. "A Strange Experience." July 30, 1876.

———. "The Woman Annie Rabourne…" August 14, 1870.

Louisville Journal. "A Ghost Story." April 20, 1868.

Stacy, Helen Price. "Story of the Irish Peddler Is Remembered in Eastern Kentucky." In *Early History of Morgan County, Ky.*, ed. Mrs. E.G. McGinnis, n.p., 1977.

6. Prognosticated Passings

Louisville Courier-Journal. "Bowling Green." June 13, 1874.

———. "The *Bowling Green Pantagraph*…" March 5, 1874.

———. "*Columbia Spectator*." November 18, 1875.

———. "Dream Father Drowned Verified." March 25, 1934.

———. "Foresees His Death." April 16, 1908.

———. "Forewarned by Strange Vision." July 12, 1909.

———. "Four Years After Wife." September 30, 1909.

———. "*Henderson News*." October 21, 1874.

———. "His Last Ride." January 13, 1911.

———. "Last Wish Gratified." April 27, 1908.

———. "The *Lebanon Clarion*…" July 18, 1869.

———. "Little Ellie Stewart…" February 4, 1874.

———. "Meets Death in Railroad Accident…" August 6, 1909.

———. "Mrs. Mary Walker Bell…" January 16, 1873.

———. "Singular Premonition." February 15, 1871.

———. "Singular Presentiment." July 1, 1870.

———. "Strange Incident in the Death of a Former Warren County Politician." April 1, 1873.

Louisville Journal. "Death of an Aged Pauper." December 21, 1865.

———. "On Tuesday…" July 25, 1850.

———. "Singular and Mysterious Presentiment." January 22, 1850.

7. Morbid Miscellany

Broom, Brian. " 'She Has No One to Pray Over Her': Lady in Red Remains a Mississippi Mystery. Who Is She?" *Mississippi Clarion Ledger*, February 9, 2021. https://www.clarionledger.com.

Decatur (IL) *Weekly Republican*. "A Shower of Needles." April 13, 1876.

Lexington Press. "Bulger." April 14, 1880.

Louisville Commercial. "Headless Skeletons Found." March 6, 1898.

Louisville Courier. "The Bardstown Affair." August 22, 1851.

———. "Disgusting Spectacle." July 17, 1858.

———. "The *Elizabethtown Intelligencer*." December 19, 1856.

———. "Expected Duel This Morning." March 3, 1855.

———. "The Grave Desecration." July 19, 1858.

———. "Letter from Mr. Simpson." August 25, 1851.

———. "Money from a Grave." May 4, 1852.

———. "Mr. Haldeman…" August 23, 1851.

———. "Not Many Months Ago" January 8, 1853.

———. "Oozed Out." March 5, 1855.

———. "Our Readers Will Be Utterly Astonished." August 20, 1851.

———. "Providential Escape." August 16, 1854.

———. "Remarkable." February 18, 1857.

———. "A Remarkable Case of Supposed Petrifaction." December 6, 1853.

———. "Remarkable Preservation of the Human Body." March 13, 1857.

———. "Robbers." June 4, 1859.

———. "A Somewhat Similar Case." October 29, 1852.

———. "Suicide of A. Irwin Lampton." June 24, 1858.

———. "We Mentioned Last Week…" May 22, 1852.

Louisville Courier-Journal. "According to the Shelby Sentinel…" November 22, 1873.

———. "The Beaver Creek Wonder." November 22, 1873.

———. "The Beer Keg Tragedy." April 2, 1869.

———. "Bodies Removed." June 10, 1910.

———. "Body Missing." December 1, 1900.

———. "The Body of an Aged Woman." March 20, 1929.

———. "Body of Man Exhumed After Forty-Seven Years." November 17, 1915.

———. "Body Preserved Forty Years." May 26, 1907.

———. "Body Twitched." October 7, 1895.

———. "The Bullitt County Tragedy." July 12, 1870.

———. "A Central Kentucky Mystery." April 19, 1874.

———. "Confessed to Forgery." November 20, 1900.

———. "A Corpse, Buried in Paducah…" September 3, 1880.

———. "Danville Doings." March 8, 1873.

———. "A Deceased Female of Doubtful Age." February 10, 1869.

———. "The *Grayson Bugle* Says." May 1, 1899.

———. "Eleven Dead Bodies…" June 12, 1872.

———. "Face Like Marble." October 31, 1907.

———. "Faithful Fido." May 4, 1873, 1.

———. "*Falmouth Independent.*" September 17, 1875.

———. "Four Bodies to Be Exhumed…" November 14, 1915.

———. "Frankfort." August 15, 1870.

———. "The *Greenup Independent.*" August 14, 1876.

———. "The *Greenup Independent.*" September 4, 1876.

———. "Harrodsburg *People*." October 4, 1873.

———. "Kentucky News." March 18, 1873.

———. "Len G. Faxon…" June 3, 1874.

———. "A Long Story." July 6, 1870.

———. "A Louisville Horror." April 1, 1869, 4.

———. "A Magnificent Hearse." January 26, 1873.

———. "Mercer Matters." February 15, 1872.

———. "Merrick's Grave." December 3, 1900.

———. "A Mysterious Skeleton." December 19, 1874.

———. "Mystery About Forger Merrick's Body…" December 2, 1900.

———. "The Negroes of Harrodsburg…" February 12, 1872.

———. "Not Yet Out of Danger." June 19, 1894.

———. "Old Coffin Is Found in Grave in Cellar." August 17, 1925.

———. "*Owensboro Examiner*." August 14, 1876.

———. "*Paris Kentuckian*." November 17, 1876.

———. "The *Paris Kentuckian*…" April 12, 1872.

———. "The People of Lexington…" April 8, 1880.

———. "Plaster Cast." September 8, 1909.

———. "Preparing for the Inevitable." April 7, 1899.

———. "The Press on L.A. Gerbier." April 3, 1869.

———. "Remains Intact." August 8, 1908.

———. "A Remarkable Case." January 11, 1883.

———. "Rites Today for Carlisle Victim." May 8, 1927.

———. "A Rose That Lived Eighteen Years in a Child's Coffin." November 21, 1873.

———. "Solid Rock Sepulcher Awaits Browder's Body." September 11, 1906.

———. "Some Unclaimed Skulls." June 21, 1874.

———. "Taken Sick at a Wake." June 18, 1894.

———. "There Were Reinterred…" November 10, 1869.

———. "Two Human Skeletons." March 6, 1898.

———. "Whether His Eccentricity…" October 16, 1872.

———. "A Witch That Was a Witch." November 14, 1871.

Louisville Daily Courier. "The Solitude and Darkness of the Mammoth Cave." October 23, 1858.

Louisville Journal. "Correction." September 25, 1865.

———. 'Mysterious and Horrible." September 22, 1865.

———. "Terrible and Swift Justice." December 14, 1865.

News-Democrat and Leader (Russellville, KY). "When It Rained Knitting Needles." May 25, 1939.

ABOUT THE AUTHOR

Keven McQueen was born in Richmond, Kentucky, in 1967. He has degrees in English from Berea College and Eastern Kentucky University and is a senior lecturer in composition and world literature at EKU. He has written nineteen books on history, the supernatural, historical true crime, biography and many strange topics, covering nearly every region of the United States. In addition, he has made many appearances on radio, podcasts and television. Look him up on Facebook or at kevenmcqueenstories.com.